THE FICTION OF **FRANK NORRIS**
THE AESTHETIC CONTEXT

DON GRAHAM

University of Missouri Press

Columbia & London, 1978

THE FICTION OF FRANK NORRIS:
THE AESTHETIC CONTEXT

Library of Congress
Cataloging in Publication Data

Graham, Don, 1940–
    The fiction of
    Frank Norris.

    1. Norris, Frank,
    1870–1902—Knowledge—Art.
I. Title.
PZ2473.G7   813'.4   77–18298
ISBN 0–8262–0252–7

Illustrations on pp. i–v reprinted
courtesy The Bancroft Library.
Illustrations on pp. 73, 96, and 98
reprinted courtesy the
Humanities Research Center,
The University of Texas at Austin.

Copyright © 1978 by
The Curators of the
University of Missouri
University of Missouri Press,
Columbia, Missouri 65211
Library of Congress Catalog
Card Number 77–18298
Printed and bound in the
United States of America

For
My
Mother
and
Father

Acknowledgments

Portions of this book have appeared in *American Literature, Papers on Language and Literature,* and *Studies in American Fiction.* I am grateful to each journal for initial publication and for permission to reuse these materials in slightly different form. I am also grateful to the American Philosophical Society for successive summer grants in 1974 and 1975 that made it possible for me to study the papers of Frank Norris and his circle at the Bancroft Library. To James D. Hart, Director of the Bancroft, and the staff there, especially Irene Moran, Head of Public Services, I am indebted for many kind services.

This book would never have reached its present stage had not Professor Max Westbrook asked the right questions at the beginning.

Catherine Callen, Kathye Self Bergin, and Carrie King provided helpful bibliographical and secretarial assistance. Sandra K. Graham was supportive every step of the way.

D. G.
Austin, Texas
3 May 1978

Contents

"Oh, speak to me of this;
speak to me of art;
speak to me of aesthetics."
—*Blix*

God! I'd rather pull the
teats of a cow than squeeze
tubes of cobalt and carmine!
—Bruce Porter

Apologia:
or, why Frank Norris?

In a recent bibliographical survey of the history of Frank Norris scholarship, Jesse Crisler and Joseph R. McElrath, Jr., pause to wonder "why, exactly, so many people—though admittedly the number is not vast—spend so much time writing about a novelist who seems to give them so little pleasure."[1] This is an excellent question to which I should like to suggest a couple of answers. First, Norris wrote a good deal of theoretical criticism, and his efforts to define major terms make him a convenient pivotal figure to study. In the debate that raged in the nineties between the forces of realism and romanticism, Norris tried to play both ends against the middle. By perceiving Zola as a romantic writer, he effectively scrambled the traditional categories of the escapist and historical romancers, who opposed not only French naturalism but Howellsian realism as well. Norris's attempt at synthesizing realism and romance into the new currency of naturalism thus makes him a textbook model of . . . something. In book-length studies he has been called a pioneer of naturalism and a scion of transcendentalism. Such contradictions are a good index of the difficulty of affixing a label to Norris's work. And we might recall that early in his career, in 1895, he said: "One is even led to regret the very invention of the terms of 'romanticism,' 'realism,' 'naturalism.' "[2]

A second reason for Norris's popularity with critics who basically don't like his work is his ideas. Norris was a writer with big ideas that are very apparent in his texts; they beg to be analyzed and to have their origins traced. The principal ideas in Norris's fiction, occurring in passages of apparently detached authorial intervention, are commonplace enough. In various novels one can find evidence of social

1. *Frank Norris: A Reference Guide*, p. xiii.
2. "Our Unpopular Novelists: Disappearance of American Fiction From The Book Stores."

1

Darwinism, biological Darwinism, atavism, degeneration, evolutionary idealism, determinism, and others. But as Donald Pizer has pointed out in an article he wrote after his influential study of Norris as a novelist of ideas, the problem with ideas in fiction is that they are too often allowed to float free of their context, to emerge as separate units of thought rather than as moments of fictive psychology associated with characters in a dense context of experience. Pizer's example from Norris is a good one. At the end of chapter 14 of *Vandover and the Brute*, a long passage of classic social-Darwinist language occurs. Read carelessly, the passage seems to reveal Norris rather simplemindedly editorializing on his theme of Vandover as helpless victim of inexorable social forces. Read carefully, as Pizer does, the passage reflects not Norris's but his hero's state of mind.[3] Social Darwinism is an image for Vandover's fear; it is important, not as a belief, but because it reveals how Vandover thinks: in the clichés of his age.

When the ideas of a novelist seem dated, those ideas are more apparent than when we, seeing current ideas in contemporary novelists whom we admire and agree with, nod approvingly in passing. Norman Mailer comes to mind. The overt thinking in *The Naked and the Dead* is only now beginning to seem just that. Readers in the late forties and fifties, looking for signs of the rise of fascism in the United States, were apt to find Mailer's thinking brilliant and prophetic. Had he advocated Lombrosian theories about born criminals, as Norris does in some of his works, nobody would have been taken in by such obviously dated ideas. Or as Gore Vidal puts it in a recent essay, talking of science in Thomas Pynchon: "But the scientific aspects of Pynchon's work will eventually become as out-of-date as those of Henry Adams. Science changes: one day we are monists, the next day pluralists. Proofs are always being disproven by other proofs. At the end, there are only words and their arrangement."[4]

3. "The Problem of Philosophy in the Novel."
4. "American Plastic: The Matter of Fiction," p. 38.

No matter how useful Norris is for defining naturalism as a fictional enterprise or for displaying classic nineteenth-century assumptions about man and reality, most critics who like him for these reasons dislike him when it comes down to the real question of his art. As an artist, Norris is barely on the literary map. Thus one critic says of a Norris novel that he thinks major: "As art *McTeague* leaves much to be desired. The novel is not likely to excite much enthusiasm among critics who cherish formal perfection."[5] And another critic, who believes that Norris's reputation is largely an "accident of publicity," provides a summary indictment of his formal crudities: "All in all, composition in Norris' novels seems to be reckoned exclusively in calculations of decibels and gross tonnage."[6] These are severe condemnations, and these critics are not alone. For a complete rundown of charges against Norris, Crisler and McElrath's study supplies a useful compendium.[7]

In the face of such disapproval, one can scarcely hope to overturn anti-Norris sentiment. Nothing that I say is going to persuade readers who think *The Ambassadors* the highest form of art that *McTeague* is its equal. (Besides, I don't think that Norris's novel is as great as James's.) But it is my opinion that Norris deserves more credit as an artist than he has received. The present study is an attempt to define and set forth the best of Frank Norris, and to try to understand what is valuable about his fictional world and what is artistically successful in his presentation of that world.

In order to accomplish these ends, a new perspective on Norris's fiction is required. Aesthetic documentation gives us that perspective. By the phrase *aesthetic documentation*, I am referring to the extensive references to all manner of art in Norris's fiction, including paintings, interior decor, drama, literature, sculpture, music, landscapes. For a novelist thought to be preoccupied with the seamier aspects of

5. Warren French, *Frank Norris*, p. 68.
6. Warner Berthoff, *The Ferment of Realism: American Literature, 1884–1919*, p. 225.
7. *Frank Norris: A Reference Guide*, p. xiii.

life—Zelda Sayre thought she had never read a smellier book than *McTeague*—Norris's works contain an extraordinary amount of highbrow aesthetic material. This dimension of his fiction has been noted in passing but has never been subjected to sustained discussion. It is, I believe, one of the keys to Norris's mind and craft.

All his adult life, Norris was keenly involved in the aesthetic atmosphere of the nineties. In 1891, for example, when he petitioned the university authorities at Berkeley for a change of status from student-at-large to special student— he wanted to be exempt from mathematics and Latin—Norris emphasized his adolescent dedication to the arts. He explained, with pardonable exaggeration: "Previous to entering the University I spent upwards of five years in Paris and in various parts of Italy and Germany studying, [*sic*] painting, gothic architecture and medieval archeology."[8] In portraying himself as an aesthete-in-training, Norris was not overstating the case too much, however. He had studied painting seriously at the Académie Julian in Paris, as William Dillingham has shown conclusively in his study of Norris's Paris years; he had visited museums and acquired a fairly technical understanding of medieval armor; he had developed an appreciation of opera; and judging from later evidence, he had gained some knowledge of architectural styles. This youthful interest in the fine arts was to form a constant part of his personal and creative life.

Norris's journalism reflects his aesthetic breadth. His contributions to the *Wave* include reviews of art exhibits, architecture, and plays; interviews with artists, dramatists, and actresses; and of course book reviews and critical essays on literature. In addition, aesthetic commentary is apt to occur in surprising contexts in his journalism. A description of a visit to the Swiss Colony vineyards in the Napa Valley, for example, contains one of his best formulations of the opposition between vital "Life" and stultifying "Art."

Beyond these tangible expressions of aesthetic interest in

8. "Frank Norris Petitions The President and Faculty of The University of California," ed. Franklin Walker.

diverse arts, there is the impressive group of artists and dilettantes whom Norris knew, in some cases as close friends, in the colorful San Francisco of the 1890s. This circle included the chief figures in the publication of the *Lark*, the little magazine that from 1895 to 1897 enjoyed a national reputation. The talents of this group were quite varied: Ernest Peixotto was a painter, illustrator, and author; Bruce Porter, a stained-glass artisan, painter, and author; Willis Polk, an architect and author; Porter Garnett, an artist and author; and Gelett Burgess, an editor, humorist, and author. In addition, Norris knew painters such as William Keith and Charles Rollo Peters, and the photographer Arnold Genthe; and he knew, by reputation at least, a host of San Francisco literary figures, including Joaquin Miller, Bailey Millard, Edwin Markham, Ambrose Bierce, Charles Warren Stoddard, Will Irwin, and Yone Noguchi. During the years 1891–1902 Norris was, with one exception, cognizant of every aesthetic tremor in San Francisco. The exception was the rise to prominence of Jack London, which occurred in the years 1899–1902, when Norris was mostly in the East.

Norris possessed what I would call the aesthetic habit of mind. He tended to approach experience from a perspective of taste and to be absorbed in presenting characters that reflected either consciously or unconsciously their cultural ambience. This is true even of McTeague, the most lowbrow hero in American literature up to 1899. Norris's preoccupation with questions of taste and with the aesthetic milieu of his time will be relentlessly before us in the pages to follow, but I should here like to demonstrate two instances of this preoccupation that reveal how completely characteristic this habit of mind is in Norris's work. The first example is from Norris's worst novel, *A Man's Woman*. The passage in question is, as it were, a second thought. In the first edition Norris described an amputation so graphically that he was asked, as he had been with the famous pants-wetting episode in *McTeague,* to write an inoffensive version. The first edition (1900) reads:

Dr. Street nodded to her, signifying that he was ready, and Lloyd, exerting her strength, pulled down upon the leg, at the same time turning it outward. The hip-joint dislocated easily, the head of the bone protruding. While Lloyd held the leg in place Farnham put a towel under this protruding head, and the surgeon, with a chain-saw, cut it away in a few strokes. And that was all—the joint was exsected.

The revised passage (1902) replaces the disturbing clinical details with material as characteristic of Norris as anything he ever wrote:

He [the Enemy, Death] had arrived there in that commonplace little room, with its commonplace accessories, its ornaments, that suddenly seemed so trivial, so impertinent—the stopped French clock, with its simpering, gilded cupids, on the mantelpiece; the photograph of a number of picnickers "grouped" on a hotel piazza gazing with monolithic cheerfulness at this grim business, this struggle of the two world forces, this crisis in a life.
   Then abruptly the operation was over.[9]

Surely Norris must have delighted in this revision, for it mocks the very taste that the first version offended, the tame conventionality of drawing-room art. The inadequacy of such art is exposed through the allegorical figure of the Enemy, which is really as much romance as death. The revised passage fictionalizes some of the principal concerns of Norris's literary criticism. In essay after essay he championed the power of romance to enliven the surface dullness of realism. The repetition of *commonplace*, also an echo from the essays, is Norris's attempt to add a new dimension to Howells's devotion to the average range of experience as realism's true sphere.

   The second example is perhaps even more revealing. In a late short story, "A Lost Story" (1903), Norris brought together Howells and conventional aesthetic representation. The story deals with a young woman novelist who reads manuscripts for a publishing firm (as Norris did when he first came to New York) and who appropriates the ideas of

9. Joseph Katz and John J. Manning reprint the two passages in "Notes on Frank Norris's Revision of Two Novels," p. 258.

a manuscript that comes across her desk. But the most interesting part of the story is the character of Trevor, who is clearly a fictionalization of Howells. Trevor is described as "This old gentleman, this elderly man of letters, who had seen the rise and fall of a dozen schools, was above the influence of fads, and he whose books were among the classics even before his death was infallible in his judgments of the work of the younger writers."[10] Clearly this writer and critic is a titan, yet Trevor has another dimension as well; he is human, down-to-earth, and as bourgeois as a Balzac novel. The presentation is quintessential Norris:

> And Trevor himself was a short, rotund man, rubicund as to face, bourgeois as to clothes and surroundings (the bisque statuette of a fisher boy obtruded the vulgarity of its gilding and tinting from the mantelpiece), jovial in manner, indulging even in slang. (p. 314)

The bisque fisherboy is Norris's shorthand transcription of the accoutrements of Gilded Age culture and the concerns of realism. The figure appears in similarly parenthetical syntax in the 1901 essay "A Plea For Romantic Fiction," where its function is to depict realism's tameness and limitations. In *Blix* (1899) it is a source of mirth for the two young lovers. But no matter how much Norris derided the bisque object for its gilded and tinted effects, he needed the fisherboy, the objet d'art, as completely as did the tradition that he felt paid too much homage to such surface detail.

When we consider Norris's complaints against realism and recall his own novels, we realize that adding another dimension to realism did not mean abandoning the commitment to cultural and aesthetic documentation. Thus he writes,

> Let Realism do the entertaining with its meticulous presentation of teacups, rag carpets, wall paper and haircloth sofas, stopping with these, going no deeper than it sees, choosing the ordinary, the untroubled, the comonplace.[11]

10. Frank Norris, *The Complete Edition of Frank Norris*, 10:300. Hereafter, all citations to "A Lost Story" are from this edition and will be included in the text.
11. "A Plea for Romantic Fiction."

The meticulous presentation of rag carpets and wallpaper is a self-characterization of Norris's own novels; although Norris wanted to go beyond objective decor, he nevertheless depended on it for a base, for a specificity and density without which novels like *A Man's Woman* drifted into abstract, simpleminded, and above all, unrealized polarities. Norris saw himself, in short, challenging American realism on its home ground, the drawing room; his fiction is a kind of dialectical engagement with the furniture of American homes and American minds. Dialectic involves synthesis, not displacement; and Norris's novels are a true effort to synthesize warring elements, to combine explorations into the "black, unsearched penetralia of the soul of man" with commonplace detail, bisque statuettes, and the like.[12]

Besides coloring much of what he thought and wrote, aesthetic experience provided Norris with a subject in perfect accord with his talent for description. At their best in Norris's fiction, descriptions of aesthetic data constitute a kind of internal, nondiscursive rhetoric of object and symbol. From his themes at Harvard to his last novel, the importance of aesthetic portraiture is unbroken. One of the Harvard themes, "A Cheap Parlor" (17 December 1894), provides vivid evidence of his skill in making such material integral to his craft. The theme describes a room that appears in two novels, *Vandover and the Brute* and *Blix*:

> The parlor was a little room with bay windows, shut off from the back parlor by sliding doors. The walls were white-washed and set off by a gilt picture-moulding. A play carpet with a reddish figures [sic] repeated innumerably upon a drab ground covered the floor. A bright green sofa with yellow cushions stood across one corner of the room. Across the opposite corner was a cheap piano. To the left of the piano a brass easel held a crayon portrait of the baby. Across one corner of the portrait was a yellow drape and drapes of various colors were hung upon the pieces of furniture. Near the piano was an Alaskan grass-basket filled the photographs [sic]. On the bay window was a marble topped table on which were a couple of albums some gift

12. Ibid.

books and a bunch of wax flowers under a glass case. The mantle-piece was of marble and had a sham grate. On one side of it was an inverted section of a sewer-pipe painted with daisies and poppies and filled with gilded cat-tails tied with a blue ribbon. Over the mantel-piece was a reproduction of Shakespeare reading to the court of Queen Elizabeth.[13]

In *Vandover* Norris used this passage, with important modifications, to describe the house of Ida Wade, the "fast" girl whom Vandover seduces and who commits suicide from despair over Vandover's apparent indifference. Norris has added nearly a hundred words to the original theme and altered the syntax somewhat. The major differences are that some details have been changed and that new ones have been added. The painting of Shakespeare at Elizabeth's court, which has ironic relevance to the low cultural level of the parlor, is dropped in favor of a "huge and striking picture, a species of cheap photogravure, a lion lying in his cage, looking mildly at the spectator over his shoulder."[14] This allusion echoes the numerous beast motifs in *Vandover* and directly recalls the hero's early desire to paint a similar canvas. New details include a clock embedded in an artist's palette embellished with gilt brushes. The pertinence of this symbol in a novel about a would-be artist is obvious. These two passages thus show very well Norris's conscious use of aesthetic detail.

But he was to use the "Cheap Parlor" material still another time, in *Blix*. Here, the principal change in the first half of the passage is the addition of a drawing of the heroine, Travis Bessemer. (In *Vandover* there is a drawing of Ida's baby sister.) The second half contains "a steel engraving of Priscilla and John Alden," an allusion befitting a novel about courtship.[15] The passage also contains that

13. *A Novelist in the Making: A Collection of Student Themes, and the Novels Blix and Vandover and the Brute*, ed. James D. Hart, pp. 72–73.

14. *The Complete Edition of Frank Norris*, 5:60.

15. *The Complete Edition of Frank Norris*, 3:14. Hereafter, all citations to *Vandover* are from this edition and will be included in the text.

ubiquitous reference in Norris's criticism and fiction, "two bisque figures of an Italian fisher boy and girl" (p. 14). The constant motif in these three versions is the bad taste of the room's decor, but Norris has modified the particularities by substituting new details pertinent to each context. For the reader familiar with Ida Wade and Blix, there would seem to be something anomalous about using the same decor to describe a "fast" girl and a pure heroine. James D. Hart has in fact observed that "this decor fits Blix rather poorly."[16] Norris was perfectly aware of the incongruity, though, as a passage later in the novel shows. Condy Rivers, the hero and suitor of Blix, launches into a playful critique of the decor, and Blix answers him in a way that explains Norris's understanding of the whole question:

> "You needn't talk about bad taste. Those drapes—oh-h! those drapes!! Yellow, s'help me! And those bisque figures that you get with every pound of tea you buy; and this, this, *this*," he whimpered, waving his hands at the decorated sewer pipe with its gilded cat-tails. "Oh, speak to me of this; speak to me of art; speak to me of aesthetics. Cat-tails, *gilded*. Of course, why not, *gilded*!" He wrung his hands. . . .
> "Oh, hush!" she interrupted. "I know it's bad; but we've always had it so, and I won't have it abused. Let's go into the dining room anyway. We've always been stiff and constrained in here." (p. 53)

Condy's raillery reveals very clearly what Norris thought of decor like this. What is equally important about the scene, though, is the heroine's simultaneous loyalty to the parlor—certainly the decor must be the work of her parents —and her dissociation from its atrocious taste. Through the successive uses of this carefully particularized room, we can see the craftsmanship that Norris brought to such materials. Rarely in his fiction did he pass up a chance to inventory a drawing room, and rarely did he fail to put such descriptions to multiple uses. Setting in Norris is always a technique for creating a sense of specific density, a way of capturing place

16. *A Novelist in the Making*, p. 73n.

and time; but it is also a method of characterization and a mode of symbolic narration.

Norris tended to think in all of his novels in terms of aesthetic opposites. This is as true of the three so-called popular novels as of the four "major" novels.[17] It is true even when there is no aesthetic documentation present! Thus *Moran of the Lady Letty* (1898), which contains no allusions to paintings, literature, or any other kind of art, exhibits the same aesthetic dialectics as appears in the copiously documented history of the nineties, *The Octopus*. The hero of *Moran*, Ross Wilbur, is a society youth who, for his future benefit and growth, is shanghaied onto a derelict privateer and forced to confront facts a good deal more coarse and elemental than afternoon tea parties. After stern tests, including killing a man, Wilbur develops into a strong, manly figure vastly superior to, and justifiably contemptuous of, his former cotillion set. In one scene, when several of his society friends come aboard Wilbur's ship, the aesthetic contrast is rendered in painterly terms:

> The three visitors—Jerry, Ridgeway, and Josie—stood nervously huddled together, their elbows close in, as if to avoid contact with the prevailing filth, their immaculate white outing-clothes detaching themselves violently against the squalor and sordid grime of the schooner's background.[18]

The extreme contrast between two kinds of experience— the naturalistic and the genteel, to use conventional terms— is paradigmatic of Norris's aesthetic vision in such works as *The Octopus*. The difference, however, lies in the much simpler solutions that *Moran* uncritically offers us: Wilbur, no artist, simply has to learn to be a man. But a figure such as Presley, the hero of *The Octopus*, who is an artist, faces

---

17. The critical standing of the popular novels is very low, to say the least; few would challenge Donald Pizer's summary of standard critical opinion: "Most critics agree that *Moran* is absurd, *Blix* slight, and *A Man's Woman* tedious" (*The Novels of Frank Norris*, p. 86). Even so, Pizer finds these works, as I do, useful as reflectors of major preoccupations in the more important novels.

18. *The Collected Works of Frank Norris*, 3:311.

far more complicated and realistic obstacles than a pack of bestial coolies, which is one of Wilbur's opponents. Still, the pattern of movement from genteel insulation to primordial experience—and back again, this being the really difficult maneuver—is identical to the problem of developing an integrative aesthetic that *The Octopus* treats at length and with much greater understanding.

In *Blix*, the most sophisticated of the popular novels, the aesthetic issue is developed with more intelligence and amplification. Here the vital opposition is not between Darwinian facts and genteel manners, but rather between drawing-room art—bourgeois, commonplace, sterile—and natural land- and seascapes—eternally original, vitalizing, restorative. The hero (Condy Rivers) and heroine (Travis Bessemer, or Blix) undergo an education in aesthetic perception. Genially scornful of the eclectic, junky bad taste of Blix's family's parlor (the description of which is a slightly modified version of the Harvard theme, "A Cheap Parlor," quoted earlier), they are drawn to a diametrically opposite mode of beauty. The scene framed by the parlor's bay window represents their aesthetic values:

> Farther than this there was nothing, nothing but a vast, illimitable plain of green—the open Pacific. But at this hour the colour of the scene was its greatest charm. It glowed with all the somber radiance of a cathedral. (p. 54)

Perceiving such vistas leads the couple to explore seascapes and country settings, as well as out-of-the-way places in the city. Here, as in *Moran*, the movement is outward, beyond the tame boundaries of parlor decor. Condy's and Blix's aesthetic education proceeds along other lines as well; under Condy's tutelage Blix comes to prefer Kipling to Marie Corelli.[19]

What is most interesting about the aesthetic dialectics of this novel is that Norris does not choose the simple solu-

19. Marie Corelli, a best-selling author of the period, combined "the appeals of Ouida and Mrs. Humphrey Ward." James D. Hart, *The Popular Book: A History of America's Literary Taste*, p. 190.

tion of leaving his young lovers happy in the idyllic heart of nature, as they are presented in several country scenes in which everything is pastorally harmonized in perfect beatitude. Instead, at the end of the novel Condy and Blix have their eyes set on New York. Their destiny, aesthetic and otherwise, lies amidst the "gray and darkening Eastern sky," rather than in the "confines of the garden," that is, in San Francisco and its lovely environs (p. 174). *Blix* thus treats in miniature the tensions and problems of the major fiction, especially the issue of an integrative aesthetic that is taken up in differing ways in *McTeague*, *The Octopus*, and *The Pit*. But only in *Blix* does Norris propose a model for the successful integration of artifice and nature, drawing rooms and outdoor scenes. Even so, the attainment of such a model lies in the future, in the adult lives of the two lovers.

A persistent argument in *Blix* is that "life was better than literature . . . an act was better than a thought" (p. 124). Such an idea, if pushed very far, cancels the need for, or possibility of, art. *A Man's Woman* pushes this idea beyond its limits, and the result is Norris's reductio ad absurdum of the rich opposition between drawing room and outdoor life that informs the other novels. *A Man's Woman* is obsessive in denying any value to art or to intellectual activities such as thinking, talking, and writing. The hero, Ward Bennett, a huge Arctic explorer, is something of an intellectual McTeague, if such a phrase is not too oxymoronic. Thus he preaches to his beloved, Lloyd Searight, of the dangers of polite culture, urging her to be "above little things, above the little, niggling, contemptible devices of the drawing rooms."[20] Bennett himself feels great discomfiture amid the constraints of civilized decor, as revealed in this passage, which could just as well belong to *McTeague*: "Never had Bennett seemed more out of place than in this almost dainty breakfast room, with its small feminine appurtenances, its

---

20. *The Collected Works of Frank Norris*, 6:94. Hereafter, all citations to *A Man's Woman* are from this edition and will be included in the text.

fragile glassware, its pots of flowers and growing plants" (pp. 113–14).

Fortunately for Bennett, there is the white Arctic, a vast nonrestrictive space commensurate with his size and needs, to save him from drawing-room captivity. His white world finds an amazing correlative in the aesthetic preferences of his fiancée, Lloyd. In a passage describing the decor of a country house that Lloyd admires, Norris presents a room disturbing in its psychological implications. The word *white* totally dominates the room ("Everything was white"), appearing no less than seven times in the paragraph (p. 79). This is too much whiteness, a whiteness devoid of sensuous possibilities. This anesthetic decor reveals a distrust of aesthetic experience more striking even than the overt fears dramatized in *Vandover and the Brute* and, more subtly, in *The Pit*. Against the commonplaceness and conventionality of drawing rooms, *A Man's Woman* has only the all-color of whiteness to offer as a counteraesthetic.

To turn from the simple antinomies of the popular novels to the four works upon which Norris's still unstable reputation rests is to encounter a fictional world rich in density of aesthetic reference and complex in thematic resolutions. Each of these novels—*Vandover and the Brute* (1914), *McTeague* (1899), *The Octopus* (1901), and *The Pit* (1903)—will require a chapter of explicative attention. To understand Norris's rhetoric of aesthetic detail, it is often helpful and sometimes imperative to understand the relationship between fiction and source, to trace aesthetic concretion in the novels to Norris's milieu, to San Francisco in the 1890s and, in particular, to the small circle of friends and acquaintances known as Les Jeunes. This group produced a diffuse but coherent body of aesthetic commentary, the main principles of which correspond closely with Norris's aesthetic ideals. There are many passages of virtually interchangeable opinion to be found among the various writings of Norris and Les Jeunes, especially Gelett Burgess, Bruce Porter, and Willis Polk. Instead of setting forth these correspondences here, I prefer to let them emerge inductively in the analyses to follow. My aim everywhere is to illuminate the fiction from within and to show, wherever appropriate, connections with the world out of which Norris developed his aesthetic theories and practice.

The Rhetoric of
Aesthetic Experience
in *Vandover and the Brute*

Norris's first novel, *Vandover and the Brute* (1914), combines elements of sensational naturalism with aesthetic documentation, creating a work of considerable subtlety and
interest.[1] Explicit naturalistic surface detail in the novel is
so obvious that most criticism has concentrated on the more
lurid aspects.[2] Another obvious and largely detrimental
characteristic of the novel is the presence of a finger-wagging
omniscient voice lecturing against self-indulgence. What
results, of course, is a strong tractarian tone. Indeed, when
a passage from *Vandover* is compared with one from *Ten
Nights in a Bar-Room*, as Warren French has done, the most
sympathetic Norris reader is hard pressed to tell the difference.[3] But despite some hectoring passages, some graceless
and bombastic moments, *Vandover* is neither a tract nor
a naturalistic melodrama. Rather the novel is an inquiry
into the nature of aesthetic experience, that complex reality
that preoccupied Norris in all his important novels.

In *Vandover* Norris seeks to demonstrate an essential

1. Bibliographical facts about *Vandover*, or the absence of facts,
have produced a good deal of disagreement about which came first,
Vandover or *McTeague*. Two critics who believe that *McTeague* was
written first are James Childs, "The First Draft of *McTeague*: 1893,"
and John S. Hill, "The Writing and Publication of the Novels of
Frank Norris," p. 151. But Donald Pizer offers convincing evidence
that *Vandover* came first. He also questions the traditional view
that Charles Norris, Frank's brother, made significant contributions
to the uncompleted text of the novel. There is no reason at present
to challenge Pizer's conclusion: "The novel, as we know it today,
was written during 1894–95, revised in 1896, and again revised, probably slightly, by Charles after Frank's death. For all practical purposes, we may consider *Vandover* as basically of 1894–95 and as
totally by Frank Norris." *The Novels of Frank Norris*, p. 33.
2. Two representative studies that stress naturalistic elements in
Vandover are: Charles C. Walcutt, "The Naturalism of *Vandover
and the Brute*," pp. 254–68; and William B. Dillingham, *Frank Norris:
Instinct and Art*, pp. 70–75.
3. *Frank Norris*, pp. 56–57.

16

qualitative difference between art and aesthetic experience, a difference that, as we shall see, throws light on the entire structure of the hero's knowledge of the world and of himself. The continuous process of definition in the novel is conducted in three rhetorical modes: authorial commentary, impressionistic point of view, and aesthetic concreteness. The first of these is akin to the tractarian voice, and in the didacticism of passages glorifying art it is easy to overlook the real content of the voice's message. For example, some passages exalt art to the skies. At various times art is called "the better half," the "strongest side of him" and the "last to go," and the "highest, most sensitive . . . of all his faculties."[4] But there are other authorial directives that identify an entirely different side of art. Vandover's compulsive attraction to prostitutes, for instance, is shown to derive from that same artistic sensibility that elsewhere is valued so highly: "Slowly the fascination of this thing grew upon him until it mounted to a veritable passion. His strong artist's imagination began to be filled with a world of charming sensuous pictures" (p. 24). Moreover, Norris also establishes an explicit connection between sensitivity—a plus—and sensuousness—a minus, at least from the tractarian, moralistic point of view—and reveals a demonic dimension of art: "It was the sensitive artist nature in him that responded instantly to anything sensuously attractive" (p. 44). Conventional readings of the novel, those that stress the hero's failure to discriminate between higher and lower feelings—between art and bestiality—simply do not take into account passages such as this one.[5] By inexorably linking Vandover's "best" impulses with his "worst," Norris demonstrates a complex deterministic causality. Also, the passage shows that to accept absolute categories of good and bad is to fall captive to the moralistic voice in

4. Frank Norris, *The Complete Edition of Frank Norris*, 5:97, 192, 213. Hereafter, all citations from *Vandover* are to this edition and will be included in the text.

5. See, for example, Stanley Cooperman, "Frank Norris and the Werewolf of Guilt," and James K. Folsom, "The Wheat and the Locomotive: Norris and Naturalistic Esthetics," pp. 65–67.

the novel and thereby to oversimplify the novel's meaning.

The same tendency to be lulled by an omniscient judgmental voice can be seen in passages rendered from an impressionistic point of view. Read carelessly, such passages look like authorial statements. The end of chapter 14, for example, which contains a paean to social Darwinism, is really from Vandover's perspective, not Norris's, as Donald Pizer has shown.[6] Another example from the same chapter shows the same device applied to the subject of art and aesthetic experience. Vandover is transported by the music of an opera (*Faust*, the same opera described in a completely different context in Norris's last novel, *The Pit*):

> For the present the slow beat and cadence of the melodies of the opera had cradled all his senses, carrying him away into a kind of exalted dream. The quarter began; for him it was wonderfully sweet, the long-sustained chords breathing over the subdued orchestral accompaniment, like some sweet south wind passing in long sighs over the pulse of a great ocean. It seemed to him infinitely beautiful, infinitely sad, subdued minor plaints recurring persistently again and again like sighs of parting, but could not be restrained, like voices of regret for the things that were never to be again. Or it was a pathos, a joy in all things good, a vast tenderness, so sweet, so divinely pure that it could not be framed in words, so great and so deep that it found its only expression in tears. There came over him a vague sense of those things which are too beautiful to be comprehended, of a nobility, a self-oblivion, an immortal eternal love and kindness, all goodness, all benignity, all pity for sin, all sorrow for grief, all joy for the true, the right, and the pure.
>
> To be better, to be true and right and pure, these were the only things that were worth while, these were the things that he seemed to feel in the music. It was as if for the moment he had become a little child again, not ashamed to be innocent, ignorant of vice, still believing in all his illusions, still near to the great white gates of life. (pp. 186–87)

This is precisely the kind of passage for which Norris has often been condemned. But it should be clear that this pas-

6. "The Problem of Philosophy in the Novel."

sage is an expression of Vandover's viewpoint, not Norris's, and that Norris in fact has distanced himself as far as possible from the sentimental clichés of Vandover's response and from his desire to embrace "illusions." There can be no doubt, I believe, that Norris is in rhetorical control of this scene. For one thing, Vandover's reaction is totally subjective. Norris reiterates the verb *seemed*; employs qualifying temporal phrases such as "for the present" and "for the moment" and qualifying conditional states such as "or" or "as if"; and constantly emphasizes *him*. Obviously Vandover imbues the music with his own psychic content, which is unrealistically vague, an impossible ethical dream. The music hardens into categorical absolutes: "all goodness," "all benignity," etc. Further, Vandover's idealized, abstracted flight leads him back to childhood with "all his illusions" intact. As we shall see, such etherealized ideas about art are exposed and criticized throughout the novel. In this passage, then, it is not Norris who is thinking sappily, but Vandover. The point I am making here is borne out by a recent critical study of *Vandover* that concentrates on another aspect, the sexual theme. Thus Joseph R. McElrath, Jr., writes of Norris's handling of hyperbole:

> He was consciously using melodramatic language derived from the lexicon of contemporary popular morality to depict the conventional mental and emotional responses of a traumatized victim of that morality. In the more melodramatic moments Norris impressionistically conforms his language to Van's consciousness, not his own response to the events that transpire in the novel.[7]

McElrath is exactly right, and this approach to Norris has to be more widely accepted if we are ever to free ourselves from the notion of Norris as a writer trapped by melodrama and see him as one capable of manipulating melodrama for more sophisticated purposes.

The third form of definition, aesthetic concreteness, is the principal rhetorical mode of the novel. Through allusion,

7. "Frank Norris's *Vandover and the Brute*: Narrative Technique and the Socio-Critical Viewpoint," p. 29.

description, and symbol, Norris provides a dramatic rhetoric of meaning that is more consistent and less inflated than the meaning conveyed in the authorial and analytical passages. Aesthetic concreteness, then, is our most reliable guide to the novel's content and power. Thus the simple dichotomies of tractarian morality are undercut by the more ambiguous contours of discrete experience, which are recorded at the most concrete level of the novel's world. There are six areas of dichotomy, or what we might better label categories of abstracted good: religion, father, the good woman, society, childhood, and art. Each is shown to be a falsification of real experience.

Vandover, it must be realized, accepts the six concepts of good without question. But the novel does not, despite some analytical and authorial passages that seem to endorse official morality. Rather, what the novel reveals beneath the surface of Vandover's unironic intellect is a strong sense of ironic exposure of the six standards of good. That is, each is subject to experiential evaluation. More than once, Vandover measures himself against the six standards; and in chapter 14, stirred by the opera, he reviews his life with reference to each. At this point his life is in considerable disarray: Ida Wade, a girl he seduced, has committed suicide; his father has died; and he feels himself adrift in idleness and dissipation. Here is Vandover's self-assessment:

> Religion could not help him, he had killed his father, estranged the girl he might have loved, outraged the world, and at a single breath blighted the fine innate purity of his early years. (p. 191)

In the light of much evidence elsewhere in the novel, this review of Vandover's "sins" reduces the complex to the simple and ignores the particularities of experience. He is thinking in the oversimplified and melodramatic abstractions of popular ethics. Vandover believes that art, the most valuable of the categories, will save him, and he sentimentalizes it into an ethical rigidity as oversimplified and unrealistic as his ideas about purity and childhood and the other abstract concepts. In his immediate effort to return to his art, there is a striking example of his inadequate understanding. His drawing produces "lines on his canvas [that] were those of a child just learning to draw" (pp. 196–97). Here childhood, elsewhere a sentimental plus, becomes a minus. Childhood thus may equal purity, but it also equals incompetence. The same scrambling of ethical categories occurs everywhere in the novel. The result is a work that requires close attention to the specificities and nuances of aesthetic reference.

For critics who accept the rhetoric of social Darwinism and tractarian morality, *Vandover* is a very tidy novel with a very clear meaning. Thus two representative critics say almost the same thing: "Norris makes it quite evident that Vandover's problem was his own dual nature and his failure to curb the evil, sensual side of that nature"[8] and "Vandover, surrendering to the sensual, will lag behind and be crushed."[9] In each case *sensual* is the key term, but it is much too narrow, inclusive, and puritan to cover Vandover's range of feeling. *Sensual* is a word Vandover would indict himself with, but the novel does not do so. The real degeneration in *Vandover* involves not surrender to feeling but rather the loss of the capacity to feel at all. Aesthetic experience is both the determinant and the measure of feeling, and Vandover falls away from feeling. *Vandover* is a study in imperception, in the incapacity of the hero to evaluate critically the nature of art and aesthetic experience.

Vandover's is a history of a poorly trained sensibility. His adolescence is an attempt to comprehend a battering array of sensuous details; his manhood is the collapse of the sensibility developed in his adolescence. From the beginning art is central to that sensibility. As a child Vandover lives in a womanless house. Of his mother, who died in the East when he was eight, he can remember only the scene of her death. His memories date from the age of thir-

8. Robert W. Schneider, "Frank Norris: The Naturalist as Victorian," p. 17.

9. Pizer, *The Novels of Frank Norris*, p. 41.

teen and from his father's house in San Francisco, where they have lived for several years. His strongest memories are of sexuality and art. Interestingly, his first introduction to sexual mystery occurs in church, where he is intrigued by the litany, "all women in the perils of child-birth" (p. 7). His curiosity aroused, he hears from some high school boys the "terse and brutal truth" (p. 7). Then, by accident and while looking for a dollar that his father has misplaced, he comes across "the long article 'Obstetrics,' profusely illustrated with old-fashioned plates and steel engravings" in the *Encyclopaedia Britannica* (pp. 7–8). This movement from traditional explanations to experiential and scientific facts is characteristic of Norris.

Vandover's interest in art develops at "about the same time"as his dawning awareness of sex (p. 8). He tries to play the piano, acts out parts of made-up plays, and writes his father a poem. But the most important contact with art occurs when he discovers in his father's library another absorbing book, " 'A Home Book of Art,' one of those showily bound books one sees lying about conspicuously on parlour centre tables" (p. 9). The "Home Book of Art" appears several times in Norris's work. In a sketch for the *Wave* in 1896, he described an art student's reliance on the work: "At home he has made fearful copies of the sentimental pictures in the 'Home Book of Art.' "[10] In *Blix* there is a comic gloss on the volume. Pretending that her friend Condy Rivers is a door-to-door salesman, Blix tells him: "Don't want to subscribe to any Home Book of Art. We're not artistic; we use drapes in our parlours."[11] In *Vandover* the contents of the "Home Book of Art" are specified in detail and ironically reflect its quality:

> There were a great many full-page pictures of lonely women, called Reveries or Idylls, ideal "Heads" of gypsy girls, of coquettes, and heads of little girls crowned with cherries and illustrative of such titles as Spring, Youth, Innocence. Besides these were sentimental pictures, as, for

10. "Western Types: An Art Student."
11. *The Complete Edition of Frank Norris*, 3:100.

instance, one entitled It Might Have Been, a sad-eyed girl, with long hair, musing over a miniature portrait, and another especially impressive which represented a handsomely dressed woman flung upon a *Louis Quinze* sofa, weeping, her hands clasped over her head. She was alone; it was twilight; on the floor was a heap of opened letters. The picture was called "Memories." (pp. 9–10)

The assumptions underlying such sketches are ones that Mark Twain's Emmeline Grangerford would appreciate: sentimentality, ideality, and melodrama. All three have lasting and disastrous effects on Vandover. Such art offers a false vision of women. Vandover thus holds from his early teens a melodramatic conception of women gleaned from two diametrically opposite images: the raw biological facts of science and the ennobling and unrealistic idealization of popular art.

The etherealized maidens of the "Home Book of Art" are not to be found in experience, however. Turner Ravis, the "good" girl who is courted by Vandover, Dolly Haight, and finally Charlie Geary, is on the surface the closest thing in the novel to the "Home Book of Art" ideal. She comes from a staid upper-middle-class family and is described as a "frank, sweet-tempered girl and very pretty" (p. 29). She reads the *Chautauquan*, surely the literary equivalent of the "Home Book of Art." Moreover, Turner is the upholder of conventional moral values and relishes making sententious statements about the proper relationship of man and woman in society. Indeed she is a fine representative of the kind of woman who was expected to set the moral tone for society in the nineties. In 1895 the *Wave* described the function of such women in an editorial: "In what is called Society men do not figure. Women constitute Society. He who seeks to gauge the moral tone of a community need not ask what the men are like; he must apply his moral thermometer to the women and inquire how they compare with members of the sex elsewhere."[12] Yet there are some disturbing aspects of Turner's character that confound the idealized picture that

12. "Is San Francisco A Sink of Iniquity?"

Vandover—and Dolly Haight in particular—hold of her. She drinks beer and likes to play poker. She has no capacity for forgiveness; when Vandover errs, she drops him completely. Most damaging of all, she accepts as suitor Charlie Geary, the most selfish and rapacious figure in the novel. Turner's last name provides an ironic clue to her doubleness; it suggests *ravish*.[13]

Turner, the abstract "good girl," has a demonic counter, the whore Flossie, the "bad girl." Flossie is a paradox of negative and positive qualities, combining coarse depravity and natural beauty. Her voice, for example, is "hoarse, a low-pitched rasp, husky, throaty, and full of brutal, vulgar modulations" (p. 45), and her profession announces itself with "her slightest action": "Her uncovered face and hands seemed to be only portions of her nudity" (p. 44). Yet Flossie, in her concrete specificity, is much more appealing than Turner Ravis and the abstract, unrealistic maidens of the "Home Book of Art": "She was an immense girl, quite six feet tall, broad and well made, in proportion. She was very handsome, full-throated, heavy-eyed, and slow in her movements" (p. 43). The most striking image that Norris employs conveys a sense of country-bred health: "Her teeth . . . were as white, as well-set, and as regular as the rows of kernels on an ear of green corn" (p. 43).

Symbolically, Flossie is a desirable, possessable Turner Ravis. The angel in the house is a pale abstraction; the fallen angel in the whorehouse is a picture of health redolent of vitality and flesh. Flossie's perfume, which arises from her body, contrasts with the "faint odour of . . . perfume" emanating from Turner (p. 176). Moreover, Flossie does not drink or play cards. Her name, a diminutive of Florence or Flora, which means "blooming" or "blossoming," is another clue to her paradoxical nature.[14] It is easy to understand Vandover's confusion in reading these women accurately

13. Walter John Bauer, who has explicated many of the names in Norris's novels, agrees that *Ravis* may be *ravish*. "The Man-Woman Relationship in the Novels of Frank Norris," p. 90.

14. Ibid., p. 67.

when we remember that one of his earliest artworks was a "life-sized Head, crowned with honeysuckles and entitled 'Flora' " (p. 11).

Besides influencing his ideas about women, the "Home Book of Art" exerts strong influences upon Vandover's painting and thus helps shape the only career he ever wants to pursue. Captivated by the sentimental maidens, Vandover tries to draw them himself. To encourage this interest, his father gives the boy a dollar as reward and hires an art teacher who, it turns out, complements perfectly the "Home Book of Art" manner. The teacher's work consists of "a conventionalized outline-picture of some kind of dove or bird of paradise, all curves and curlicues, . . . carrying in its beak a half-open scroll" upon which are written "senti-ments" (p. 10). Vandover's youthful masterpiece, "Flora," derives from the teacher's meretricious ideals and earns the boy a bigger prize, a five-dollar gold piece from his father.

The influence of the "Home Book of Art" is felt long after Vandover has advanced beyond imitations of life-size heads. To understand its harmful effect, it is necessary briefly to review Vandover's attempts to develop his paint-ing. During the Harvard years Vandover spent a summer in Maine, where, by drawing the local landscape, he began to tap some important energies: "His style improved immensely the moment he abandoned flat studies and began to work directly from Nature" (p. 21). But later, after his return to San Francisco, Vandover continues to draw Maine land-scapes. He sells one of these and receives a bonus of twenty dollars from his father. Had Vandover directed his attention to the landscape before his eyes, especially to the urban land-scape that Norris the painterly novelist describes in vivid detail, his art might have truly developed into something of value.[15] Vandover's formal training in San Francisco

15. What I have in mind is this compelling description of an urban scene: "It was a sordid and grimy wilderness, topped with a grey maze of wires and pierced with thousands of chimney stacks. Many of the roofs were covered with tin long since blackened by rust and soot. Here and there could be seen clothes hung out to dry. Occasionally upon the flanking walls of some of the larger build-

illustrates the same tendency to forsake the natural for the contrived and conventional. He studies at the School of Design, an institution founded by the San Francisco Art Association in 1874 that provided good training for many local artists in the 1890s.[16] At the school Vandover does two kinds of painting; one complements and deepens his talent, the other does not. The first kind is a study of observable nature: "The model for that week was a woman, a fact that pleased Vandover, for he drew these nude women better than any one in the school, perhaps better than anyone in the city" (p. 56). But the second kind is very derivative; these paintings typically dramatize an experience and landscape alien to Vandover's knowledge: a lion in the Sahara desert, or a dying war-horse on a vast plain. Vandover's source is obviously the French Academicians, with Jean Léon Gérôme being the most probable specific influence, as William B. Dillingham has shown in detail.[17] Although these paintings are "effective," this tradition leads Vandover in no useful or vital directions (p. 54). The masterpiece that he envisions is never finished, and Norris makes an essential connection between this projected work, a study of a dying cavalryman in a desert with a lion moving in upon him, and Vandover's earlier art: "The melodrama of the old English 'Home Book of Art' still influenced Vandover. He was in love with this idea for a picture and had determined to call it 'The Last Enemy' " (p. 54). It should be clear that this painting does not represent a significant gain in Vandover's development. Norris's other comments on the Academicians support a

---

ings was displayed an enormous painted sign, a violent contrast of intense black and staring white amidst the sooty brown and grey, advertising some tobacco, some newspaper, or some department store" (*The Complete Edition of Frank Norris*, 5:236).

16. For a history of the organization, see John I. Walter, "The San Francisco Art Association," p. 98.

17. *Frank Norris: Instinct and Art*, p. 12. Although Dillingham makes some interpretive points about art in the fiction, mainly he is concerned to show how certain attitudes of the Academicians—hard work, close observation, careful research, and good draftsmanship—influenced the young Norris's developing conception of both painting and writing.

similar criticism of this school. In a review for the Art Association Exhibit at the Hopkins House in 1897, for example, he pointed out the "tame mediocrity" of a Detaille.[18] His satirical sketch of an art student, published in the *Wave* in 1896, is another indication of critical distance. The student's limited abilities are shown in his reliance on both the "Home Book of Art" and on Adolphe William Bouguereau, one of the most famous Academicians and Norris's teacher in France: "Bouguereau is his enthusiasm; he can rise no higher than that, and he looks down with an amused smile upon the illustrators, the pen-and-ink men, Gibson, Smedley, Remington, and the rest."[19] Norris's sense of Bouguereau's shortcomings is all the more clear when we realize that he greatly admired the work of Gibson and Remington.[20] The sketch and the novel suggest that by 1896 Norris had come to see the Academic tradition as very similar to the popular art of the "Home Book of Art." Both traditions depended upon melodramatic extrapolation from observable reality, and neither offers Vandover a viable mode of perception.

Vandover's career as a landscape artist is brought to a wonderful conclusion by his last job as an artist, drawing prescribed and grotesque landscapes on safes. The alliance between bad art and economic power could hardly be more effectively joined, nor could Vandover's talents be more minimized than in such efforts as "those little oval landscapes between the lines of red and gold lettering—landscapes, rugged gorges, ocean steamships under all sail, mountain lakes with sailboats careening upon their surfaces" (p. 276). The symbolic connections between art and money deserve careful attention. It will be recalled that Vandover's father rewards his son's artistic efforts with cash. Money is the father's central criterion of value. Almost sixty when the

18. "Art Association Exhibit: Fall Work of the Local Artists on View at the Hopkins House."

19. "Western Types: An Art Student."

20. See Norris's reviews, "A Question of Ideals: The American Girl of 1896 as Seen by Wenzel and by Gibson" and "Holiday Literature: The Chinese and California Girl Calendars—Remington's Great Sketches."

novel opens, the father, who is nearly always tagged with the epithet "Old Gentleman" or "Governor," is a businessman who "had lost the capacity for enjoying anything but the business itself" (p. 3). For him art is decidedly a peripheral matter, and though he has money "to cultivate a taste for art, music, literature, or the drama, to indulge in any harmless fad," he prefers instead to stave off boredom by becoming a developer of "little houses and cheap flats" (p. 4). In one of those happy symbolic moments that capture the essence of a character, Norris describes a ritualistic act of the Old Gentleman's:

> On the first of each month when his agents turned over the rents to him he was in great spirits. He would bring home the little canvas sack of coin with him before banking it, and call his son's attention to the amount, never failing to stick a twenty-dollar gold piece in each eye, monocle fashion, exclaiming, "Good for the masses," a meaningless jest that had been one of the family's household words for years. (p. 4)

Far from meaningless, *Good* is an ablaut pun; it stands for both *God* and *gold*, the point being that gold is the Old Gentleman's God. This submerged religious symbolism supports the alliance between economic power and religious conventionality seen in other transactions. The Old Gentleman pays his son as reward for reading the Bible on Sunday afternoons; Turner Ravis is a steady churchgoer.

Although it is clear that the Old Gentleman is being ironically exposed, critics have accepted him at face value, seeing him as allegorically representing the home[21] and as "undeniably admirable in a soft and gentle way."[22] But the Old Gentleman's official goodness is strongly undercut by the effect his values have upon his son. As we have seen, the father attaches a strictly financial value to every artistic act of his son's. He also uses an economic argument, a recent financial slump (doubtless the depression of 1894), to avoid sending Vandover to Paris, when in fact the reason is the

21. Pizer, *The Novels of Frank Norris*, p. 43.
22. Dillingham, *Frank Norris: Instinct and Art*, p. 7.

father's deep-seated puritan distrust of a foreign city where his son would be "exposed to every temptation" (p. 12). The irony of this decision is underscored by what happens to Vandover at Harvard, the father's preference over Paris. There Vandover debauches himself with the first "chippie" in sight and falls under the influence of the capitalist and future real-estate developer Charlie Geary, destined to become Vandover's father surrogate. When the Old Gentleman dies, Vandover rifles his father's most sacred possession, the savings box. In it he finds, among other things, "twenty-dollar gold pieces, the coin that used to be 'Good for the Masses' " (p. 140). Vandover is the true son of his father's values, and his last act as an artist, painting on safes, is the logical result of the kind of art his father commissioned.

Vandover's job as a safe painter, which precedes his final degradation in the rented cottage owned by Charlie Geary, occasions an interesting remark. He says, "When you paint on steel and iron your colours don't dry out true; all the yellows turn green" (p. 292). Here Vandover half recognizes for himself the subversion of art by economic power. The color green provides another symbolic link with other transactions between art and money that he is never aware of, however. Lawyer Field, who for a time after the Old Gentleman's death handles Vandover's legal affairs, possesses significant green objects: "Green cloth bags filled apparently with books, padlocked tin chests, and green pasteboard deed-boxes" (p. 141). Green is one of the colors in Vandover's lavishly decorated hotel quarters, and as his decline accelerates, green is used to symbolize that decline. His hat turns from black to a "greenish hue" (p. 280). Finally, in the cottage that Geary has hired him to clean, Vandover confronts a revolting green emblem of decay, "an old hambone covered with a greenish fuzz" (p. 308). The logical development of such motifs is evidence enough that Norris's surface data in this novel are scarcely the random notations of a careless writer.

Thus far we have looked at how certain official sanctions —childhood purity, the good girl, the father, religion, and above all, art—are exposed by experiential facts and shown to be unrealistic reductions of the total complexity of experience in the novel. But the most extensive pattern of aesthetic reference and imperception remains to be traced. This pattern, of houses and rooms, reflects derivative, conventional, and false tastes as well as a fatal imperception on Vandover's part. He fails to see and understand the interrelatedness of feeling and art. His fate is to move from a state of feeling to one of unfeeling, from a sensuous response to the world to indifference and blank incomprehension.

The successive houses and rooms inhabited by Vandover register with photographic detail his movement along the gauge of feeling. An early contrast is established between Turner Ravis's house (and Vandover's father's—together these constitute *the* middle-class house) and the Imperial Bar. The first is a Victorian house, the second a whorehouse. Significantly, not much about the Ravis decor is specified. Unidentified oil paintings, steel engravings, and old-fashioned chromos hang on the walls; the furniture is "solid, conservative"; the interior decor suggests "individuality" and preference for "old things" (p. 68). What is important here is the level of endorsement, which is quite abstract, quite official. Like Turner, the Ravis interior has very little sensuous concreteness. It also has no power of attraction. The Ravis house represents exactly what Turner does: staid, old-fashioned, and chaste conservatism, the essence of gentility.

In marked contrast is the Imperial, a counterhome for the young society men. Its decor is elaborately reported and is in both quantity and depth of sensuous detail radically different from the Ravis house. Thus we know what paintings and art objects it contains: "A large copy of a French picture representing a *Sabbath*, witches, goats, and naked girls whirling through the air," "a vase of wax flowers under glass," a "second 'bar-room' picture, representing the ladies of a harem at their bath," and so on (pp. 36–37). These erotic and bacchanalian motifs are the obverse of Turner Ravis and the "Home Book of Art" gypsies, coquettes, and ideal heads. The decor of the Imperial is a major part of its compelling power; it can draw Vandover and his friends from the safe and sterile atmosphere of the Ravises. Once after attending a stiff, genteel party at the Ravises, the young men remove to the Imperial, where the atmosphere is different, more relaxed, freer. But the reality of the Imperial is also coarser and potentially more destructive than the *Chautauquan* version in force at the Ravishes. The Imperial involves risk and intensity; the Ravis house, safety and constraint. Above all, the Imperial involves sensuous contact with the world.

The Imperial comes to have special symbolic importance for Vandover. He measures his fall from art by his allegiance to the Imperial. In a characteristically oversimplified dichotomy, the Imperial is sin and Paris is art. If he could have gone to Paris instead of always having gone to the Imperial, everything would have been different. The last time he mentions Paris he projects his fantasy further, saying that he spent the last of his money (which in fact he gambled away) to send a young artist there on the pilgrimage he himself never made. But would Paris have saved Vandover? Hardly. What he fails to realize is that Paris and the Imperial are not opposites. Rather, they share a common fund of sensuous reality, the accurate perception of which can make a person an artist and a man.

A third house in Vandover's experience is that of Ida Wade, the "fast" girl whom he seduces and whose suicide precipitates the changes in Vandover's economic situation that force him out of his father's house. In high school Ida Wade was the companion of Turner Ravis, but since then she has been ignored by "girls of that class" (p. 58). She belongs to the lower middle class, a full level below Vandover's status. Her family home parodies Vandover's father's house, which has two stories, bay windows symmetrically divided by the front door, a "sort of balcony that no one ever thought of using," and a "large well-kept yard" (p. 27).[23]

23. In "Frank Norris," James D. Hart has pointed out that Norris's family home at 1822 Sacramento Street was obviously the model for the Vandover house.

The Wade house, which has a "microscopical front yard," is given the kind of attention that characterizes most of Norris's descriptions of execrable taste:

> The parlour and front room on the second floor were furnished with bay windows decorated with some meaningless sort of millwork. The front door stood at the right of the parlour windows. Two Corinthian pillars on either side of the vestibule supported a balcony; these pillars had iron capitals which were painted to imitate the wood of the house, which in its turn was painted to imitate stone. (p. 59)

While the Wade house clearly parallels some features of the Vandover house, including having two stories, bay windows, and parlor, certain details of the superior house have been intensified and made grotesque in the Wade imitation. The nonfunctional elements of the larger house (the unused balcony) are intensified in the "meaningless" millwork and Corinthian pillars of the smaller, an instance of pseudoclassicism. There is a striking congruity between this passage and descriptions of similar houses by Ernest Peixotto, a painter and close friend of Norris, as is evidenced, for example, by Peixotto's description of the tract housing prevalent in San Francisco in the early nineties: "The facade was divided into two perpendicular sections, one being occupied by the bay windows, the other by the porch, supported by fluted Corinthian columns and crowned by a single double window."[24] Norris and all of Les Jeunes shared a strong distaste for nonfunctional design. They also shared a dislike for the use of imitative and inorganic materials. Peixotto condemned this practice in terms nearly identical to the passage in *Vandover*. Attacking "cheap and tawdry display," he bemoaned the fact that "houses of wood masquerade as stone, stucco is cut in rustic to look like granite, galvanized iron is made to match with stucco."[25]

The Wade interior, described in even more lavish detail, exemplifies further the violation of the aesthetic criteria held dear by Norris and Les Jeunes. Since the original ver-

24. "Architecture in San Francisco," p. 461.
25. Ibid., p. 450.

sion of this passage has been quoted in the introduction (see pp. 8–9), there is no need to reproduce the revision here. The Wade parlor commits three aesthetic sins. One is the inorganic mixing of the real and the artificial, which results in a contradictory state of conflicting modes. The attempt in the exterior to make iron appear as wood is matched in the interior by the easel of imitation brass. Gilded cattails are another instance of this same inappropriateness. The photogravure of the lion framed by "real iron bars, with real straw" represents a second aesthetic blunder (p. 60). It objectifies a distinction that Norris made again and again in his critical essays: the difference between the actual and the true. This piece of art errs in combining the actual—real iron, real straw—with the potentially true—the drawing of the lion. In one essay Norris uses a painting of a horse by the French Academican Édouard Detaille to illustrate the aesthetic principle of illusion: "The horse is not blue, nor has he any blue spots. Stand at the proper distance and the blue smear resolves itself in the glossy reflection of the sun, and the effect is true."[26] The third aesthetic fault is perhaps the most obvious of all: the Wade interior is cluttered, crowded, and junky. It lacks simplicity, one of the cardinal tenets of Norris and Les Jeunes.[27]

Typical of Norris at his best, this passage, besides being interesting for its inherent aesthetic elements, also serves important symbolic purposes by forecasting Vandover's future. The sewer pipe painted with daisies suggests Vandover's job of painting landscapes on safes, his eventual

---

26. "A Problem in Fiction: Truth Versus Accuracy."

27. The doctrine of simplicity is echoed everywhere in the writings of Les Jeunes. Two examples can suffice. Willis Polk, the architect and contributor to the *Lark*, identifies the "first three aristic precepts" as "simplicity, dignity, and refinement" ("The 'Artists' Choice,' or, Why the Hibernia Bank and the Huntington House Are the Most Beautiful Buildings in San Francisco"). Similarly, Gelett Burgess makes simplicity central to his aesthetic canon: "Good taste proselytizes very slowly, but one of its first lessons is that of simplicity; that useless and meaningless ornament has no place in art" ("Architectural Shams: The Efforts of San Francisco Architects to Achieve the Impossible").

sewer existence, and his last job of cleaning beneath the sink in the rental house. The broken clock that runs too fast and the mock artist's tools, the palette in which the clock is "perversely set," foretell Vandover's accelerating rush toward ruin and his concomitant inability to paint (p. 60). The lion in the photogravure recalls the lion in Vandover's uncompleted painting, "The Last Enemy," and connects with other beast motifs in the novel.[28] Examples include a Look Out for the Dog sign in the front yard of Vandover's paternal home; Vandover's own dog, who ironically bears a human name, Mr. Corkle; the Assyrian bas-relief of a wounded lioness that adorns his first apartment; his lycanthropy, the most blatant expression of the motif; and the bulldogs and mastiffs that he paints on the safes.

There is nothing so vividly redolent of bad taste in the novel as the Ida Wade parlor. Yet there is no corrolary between bad taste and Ida's ethical conduct, just as there is nothing inherently demonic about the Imperial, despite an allegorically red-eyed waiter and pictures of witches on the walls. Moreover, Turner Ravis's ethical stature, as we have seen, is undercut in several subtle ways, although otherwise she has the most impeccable credentials of gentility. Norris's treatment of taste and ethics is therefore much more complicated and interesting than is the attitude of his friend Gelett Burgess. In an essay in 1897 Burgess, lamenting bad taste in architecture, marries taste and ethics:

> For as the women seek to counterfeit the charms denied them, by the use of rouge and enamel, so the men daub and spatter redwood to imitate marble and granite, copy wood-carving by machinery, and carry the deception of concrete and cement to indecent limits.[29]

Norris's method is quite different; everywhere he seeks to scramble such easy ethical gradations. Flossie the prostitute

28. Dillingham makes an acute interpretive point about this painting: "But instead of creating the lion on canvas, which would have saved him, he [Vandover] releases it within himself and it devours him" (*Frank Norris: Instinct and Art*, p. 12).

29. "Architectural Shams."

is a strapping figure of health and vitality (when first seen; eventually she is made to conform to the conventional picture of the broken-down syphilitic hag); Turner the good girl is last seen in the company of the most rapacious character, Charlie Geary; Ida Wade, a "fast" girl, has "nothing vicious about her" (p. 58). It is imperative to understand that Ida Wade's seduction cannot be blamed on the wretched taste of her family's parlor, or on the fact that her mother produces such kitsch art as "a bunch of yellow poppies painted on velvet and framed in gilt" (p. 76), or on Ida's rather garish dress. Her seduction should be blamed, rather, on the same appeal that lures Vandover, on the sensuous reality of the Imperial, where the seduction takes place. She is as much seduced by the sensuousness of the Imperial, its champagne and oysters and the "whiff of the great city's vice" as she is by Vandover (p. 67). This is to say also that she is alive in a way that Turner Ravis never is.

It is pertinent too that the best young man in the novel, Dolly Haight, and the worst, Charlie Geary, are both defined by a singular lack of the capacity to feel or experience aesthetic contact with the world. Dolly is the only male virgin in sight (and thus the most ardent worshipper of Turner, whom he regards as a mother or sister), and he is tasteless, without sensuous drives, a dolly.[30] Geary, a shrewd capitalist and practicing social Darwinist, is almost as tasteless as Dolly, except that, like Vandover, he appreciates food. Dolly winds up with syphilis incurred from a single kiss from the tainted lips of Flossie; Geary may very well win Turner Ravis in the end; but neither represents a positive model. Dolly is too pale and weak, a cardboard cutout of virtue; and Geary is a dehumanized example of economic rapacity. Between these two extremes, these neuters of aesthetic capacity and feeling, lies Vandover, a man of feeling.

Human complexity in this novel is defined as a capacity to feel, and a character's taste functions as a barometer of

30. Stanley Cooperman has made essentially the same point: "ultimately Vandover, the doomed artist, is an adult while Haight is an infant" ("Frank Norris and the Werewolf of Guilt," p. 257).

his ability to feel, as a way to measure the stages of his growth or decline. We have already traced several such patterns, but the most sustained and elaborate evaluation of Vandover's perceptions is seen in the series of rooms that he inhabits after his father's death. The sequence begins when Vandover visits Lawyer Field's office and learns the startling fact that the cost of maintaining his father's house is prohibitive. But the most compelling fact about the visit is the pleasantness of the lawyer's room. To Vandover the lawyer's decor is much more real than the abstract economics outlined by the lawyer. Field's room, a "huge apartment," contains "walls . . . covered with rough stone-blue paper, forming an admirable background to small plaster casts of Assyrian *bas-reliefs* and large photogravures of Renaissance portraits" (p. 141). Once the house is disposed of, Vandover begins to dream of his new dwelling, adding to the lawyer's decor one specification only: "The walls covered with rough stone-blue paper. . . . and photogravures of Velasquez portraits" (p. 148). Nowhere is Vandover's derivative taste more evident.

Casting about for an appropriate place, Vandover encounters two alternatives, an apartment with a large studio and a small sitting room, or the reverse. He rejects the first one, formerly the home of an artist, on aesthetic, psychological grounds: "There did not seem to be any suitable place for the Assyrian *bas-reliefs,* and the mantelpiece was of old-fashioned white marble like the mantelpiece in Mrs. Wade's front parlour, a veritable horror" (p. 151). The same impulse that draws him to art, the need for sensuousness, makes him susceptible to the appeals of the second apartment. Located in a hotel replete with the latest conveniences, this apartment has "well-lighted spaces on the walls for casts and pictures" and a pleasing mantelpiece (p. 151). Sensuous comfort, which directly appeals to his aesthetic sensibility, proves stronger than the discipline offered by the artist's apartment. The room seduces Vandover. His submission is exactly like Ida Wade's, a gravitation toward physical delight rather than a violation of abstract principle.

Vandover's room in the comfortable hotel is a bower of pleasure. It incorporates the essence of his tastes and needs, combining objects from all the houses and rooms that have thus far made up his life. The description of the apartment, which is several pages long, contains the most extensive catalog of aesthetic detail in the novel. Here I shall indicate only a few of the details, the ones most pertinent to the rest of the novel. The room reproduces, in the color of its wallpaper and in its Renaissance paintings, Lawyer Field's decor. Among the numerous objects are casts of animals by Emmanuel Fremiet and Antoine Barye,[31] Donatello's *Femme Inconnue*,[32] a satin slipper of Flossie's, the Old Gentleman's revolver, a dozen grotesque plaster heads, a lampshade given Vandover by Turner Ravis, Assyrian bas-reliefs including one of a wounded lioness, Rembrandt's *Night Watch*, the Mona Lisa, a Velásquez, a Vandyke of a Dutch lady, and photographs of actresses and chorus girls (pp. 155–56). Here Vandover is truly revealed as a "cluster of appurtenances," a composite of the aesthetic data of his life to this moment.[33] His father's chair and revolver, Flossie's slipper, Turner's gift, all these are combined and subordinated to the latest influence, Lawyer Field's interior.

In contrast to the cluttered, junky effect of the Wade parlor, Vandover's room represents the ideal of tasteful design in fashion in the early nineties. *Early* is important here, because before the decade was over, a countermovement toward simplicity and uncluttered spareness of decorative objects was well under way; indeed, we can see an extreme difference between Vandover's room and that of the artist Presley in *The Octopus*, published in 1901. In the early nineties the trick was to bring numerous and disparate

31. Antoine Louis Barye's favorite animal subjects were lions and tigers. See, for example, the reproductions in Gerard Hubert and Maurice Serullaz, eds., *Barye: Sculptures, Peintures et Aquarelles*.

32. No listing of a Donatello work called *Femme Inconnue* appears in Luigi Grassi, *All the Sculpture of Donatello*. None of the works resemble the subject in the Norris reference.

33. The phrase is spoken by Madame Merle in Henry James's *The Portrait of A Lady*, p. 172.

objects into some kind of color and spatial harmony. A *Wave* short story of 1891 provides an excellent gloss on the kind of decor Vandover has selected for his room:

> If taste can be shown anywhere, it certainly can be in an artist's studio. There is where the immense possibilities of the arrangement of *bric-a-brac*, of falling draperies, of *chiaroscuro*, of curtains, or portieres, of the numberless incidents which go to make up that most indefinable of all things—effect—can be taken advantage of to the utmost extent. A helmet, shield, and battle-axe grouped upon some antique chest in a corner, a bust on a pedestal, some tapestries against a wall, a flower-pot or two of plants or ferns, a Japanese screen—anything or everything, in short, suggestive of art or beauty can be so arranged as to impress the senses with lofty idealism, whereas if incongruously set together, the self-same objects are calculated to excite an irritating train of thought.[34]

One can think of no finer example of the period's habit of connecting art and mind, interior decor and psychological states. Vandover's decor combines both lofty idealism and irritating trains of thought; but under the influence of both, Vandover perceives only the first. He fails to see that the decor objectifies the merger of forces symbolized by apparent opposites. This merger is effected most clearly in the profuse allusions to women. Flossie, Turner Ravis, the grotesque heads, the girl in Rembrandt's *Night Watch*, Mona Lisa, the Vandyke lady, and the actresses are all subsumed under the rubric of *femme inconnue*: unknown woman. Woman expresses a duality: heaven and hell. The Mona Lisa is a paradigm of the dilemma. It is entirely appropriate that Vandover have this painting in his room. For the nineteenth-century imagination Mona Lisa was a profoundly dualistic symbol. If she meant spirituality, she also meant sensuality. Later, when Vandover has lost most of his aesthetic possessions, he hangs upon the walls of his furnished room signs lettered "Mona Lisa" and "Stove." But the signs are not opposites; both signify a common sensuous reality; both stand for forms of energy.

34. Robert Duncan Milne, "The Artist's Spectre."

By this point we should not be surprised to learn that even Vandover's stove is "artistic," containing "flamboyant ornaments" (p. 159). Thus the stove not only ministers to Vandover's elementary need for bodily heat, it also fulfills a complementary need for aesthetic pleasure. He spends hours looking at the scenes adorning the stove's sides, but typically the implications are lost upon him. "The Punishment of Caliban and His Associates" is a pointed allusion to Vandover's sensuous experiences in the company of friends like Ellis and Dummy. "Romeo and Juliet" and the "Fall of Phaeton" are more general allusions, to the tragedy of sexual passion and to the classic fable of rise and fall.

This apartment marks the high point of Vandover's aesthetic surroundings. It also marks his characteristic failure of perception. Immersed in a comfortable life, he fails to recognize three important facts: to maintain the apartment, he needs money; to produce art, even poor-quality "Home Book of Art" stuff, he needs to work; and to grow intellectually and emotionally, he needs to understand his own self-defined milieu, the interior decor of his mind. Failing in all three respects, he is easy prey for Charlie Geary. When Ida Wade's father initiates a lawsuit and when Geary, acting for both sides, cheats Vandover out of a large sum of money, the downward slide begins.

The series of rooms inhabited by Vandover after his eviction measures a steady decline in feeling. Leaving the nice apartment requires abandoning all the things that have made his life there engrossing: "The lovely bric-à-brac, all the heavy pieces, all the little articles of *vertu* which he had bought with such intense delight and amongst which he had lived with such happiness, such contentment, such never-failing pleasure" (p. 238). His next address is a room in the Lick House, a well-known but declining hotel in the nineties. Commercially ascetic, this room lacks sensuous effects. Severe, "bare of any personality," it is a cold parody of the warm, cosy, personalized rooms to which Vandover has been accustomed (p. 237). The center table holds ice water; the mantelpiece is of iron; blank whiteness is the dominant color; the pieces of furniture have a manufactured "family resemblance" (p. 237). The name of the hotel is nicely ambiguous: _Lick_ suggests an animal image, an echo of the beast motif perhaps, but the room itself lacks anything of the animal.

The plainness and sterilized dullness of the Lick House bother Vandover at first, so much so that he imaginatively refurbishes the room: "His indulgent, luxurious character continually hungered after subdued, harmonious colours, pictures, ornaments, and soft rugs" (p. 245). He decorates it in his mind's eye exactly the way the luxurious apartment was. His declining capacities to feel and perceive are brought together most effectively in a scene that presents the ultimate insensitivity as pure unconsciousness. Characteristically, the aesthetic dimension is an integral part of the scene: "Naked, exhausted, Vandover slept profoundly, stretched at full length at the foot of the bare, white wall of the room beneath two of the little placards, scrawled with ink, that read, 'Stove here'; 'Mona Lisa here' " (p. 273). The linkage of stove and art mirrors his former requirements of animal comfort and aesthetic pleasure. The signs are bare abstractions of the energies they represent, and Vandover is here even unconscious of the signs. Another symbolic rendering of the defeat of perception is Vandover's friend Dummy. A deaf-mute, Dummy is the perfect alter ego for Vandover on the decline: the groping, unperceiving, inarticulate being at a loss to understand the world. It should be apparent by now that even Vandover's lycanthropy, a sensational way to dramatize the ravages of syphilis, is important more for its psychological effects than for its physiological ones.[35]

Finally, Vandover has to leave the Lick House with its placards of former aesthetic splendor. He moves into the Reno House, a hotel still lower on the scale. His room there is deplorable; the original version of this description, a Harvard theme, was entitled "Misery,"[36] a title that well

35. For a full discussion of the connection of lycanthropy with syphilis, see Pizer, _The Novels of Frank Norris_, pp. 36–39.
36. For the original theme, see _A Novelist in the Making: A Col-_

indicates the dominant impression arising from the details. Though this room contains more objects than the furnished room in the Lick House, they are unpleasant, grotesque. Carboniferous wallpaper reflects the aesthetic distance between this room and the grand hotel room Vandover once enjoyed. The rug is dirty; newspapers are stuck to the ceiling; the furniture is old and nondescript. One personal object present in the room is Vandover's color box, which he uses to paint the little landscapes on safes. Ironically, Vandover is now a working artist, and this bleak and dirty room is a parody of an artist's domicile.

Of course Vandover loses this room too. At one point he is seen by Ellis, who along with others of Vandover's former acquaintances believed him dead, "near the Barbary Coast, looking at the pictures in the illustrated weeklies that were tacked upon the showboard on the sidewalk in front of a stationer's" (p. 277). When he seeks out Geary for help, he is a grotesque version of the stereotypical artist: "The gaunt, shambling figure with the long hair and dirty beard, the greenish hat, and the streaked and spotted coat" (p. 289). Nothing can touch Vandover now, neither beauty nor comfort nor foulness. He is at the end of the line, a cipher, a register of nothing. The declension of houses is complete when Vandover stands alone in Geary's empty rental house. The young man who was once revolted at a mantelpiece now finds nothing abhorrent in sewer filth.

The last image of the novel reveals Vandover in a deeply ironic relation to his past. He is discovered in the cheap rental house by a child of the family who will be moving in. Vandover observes the child eating bread, but he observes him without understanding what the child objectifies: Vandover's lost state of pristine innocence. This scene brings to a conclusion a succession of child images. In the newspaper listing Ida Wade's suicide, the item next to this entry is "an advertisement of a charity concert for the benefit of a

lection of *Student Themes and the Novels Blix and Vandover and the Brute*, ed. James D. Hart, pp. 83–84.

home for incurable children" (p. 89). One of the two books that Vandover reads during the novel is about a boy at the time of Christ. A "childish desire" impels Vandover to confess his seduction of Ida Wade to his father (p. 93). Childhood always means a great deal to Vandover; at one point, when he can still think, it means everything he has lost.

Art, Vandover's quintessential need, is also equated with childhood. When he loses the ability to draw, we are told: "For this last calamity was like the death of a child of his, some dear, sweet child, that might have been his companion throughout all his life" (p. 203). This language fairly drips with sentimentality, and Vandover's linking of art and childhood here is precisely the kind of sappy, melodramatic emotionalism that characterizes his thinking throughout the novel. Finally, in an analytic passage, Norris dramatizes Vandover's paralysis of talent with a child image: "The lines on his canvas were those of a child just learning to draw; one saw for what they were intended, but they were crude, they had no life, no meaning. The very thing that would have made them intelligible, interpretive, that would have made them art, was absent" (pp. 196–97). Clearly, childhood provides no mode for living in a world of flowing and contradictory experience.

By the end Vandover is ironically a good boy, which is what he has sentimentally always wanted to be. As certification of this fact, he accepts a quarter tip from the father whose house he is cleaning for Geary. With the capacity to feel burned out of him and with all his aesthetic contact with the world rendered blank, Vandover can at last serve the five sanctions of propriety well, because the sixth, art abstracted from real experience, is no longer a possibility. Far from being a social-Darwinist or deterministic tragedy, *Vandover and the Brute* is a tragedy of the reification of experience into unrealistic and deadening rigidities of behavior. It is a tragedy of imperception, not of forces greater than the self.

Art and Humanity in *McTeague*

Until recently, *McTeague* (1899) has typically been seen as a purely naturalistic novel embodying such standard assumptions as sexual determinism, atavistic degeneracy, the influence of sordid milieus, and the operation of chance.[1] There is no question that quasi-scientific theorizing is one side of *McTeague*. Like Theodore Dreiser and Jack London, Norris often chose to ground his fiction in the presumably authoritative scientific opinion of the day. (The difference between this faith and a present-day novelist's reliance upon postexistential assumptions is slight.) Still, there is no reason to believe that Norris and the other naturalists were preoccupied with content and truth to the point of not caring about the art of fiction. Recent criticism of *McTeague,* which represents the most lively evaluation of Norris's accomplishment to occur in years, is impressive because critics have begun to approach the novel from new perspectives and without the tedious repetition of naturalistic shibboleths. Thus, critics are examining the tonal variations that create both comic and compassionate effects, the image patterns, and the appropriation of Dickensian methods in exploring lower-class life, all of which testify to the novel's craftsmanship and humanity.[2] McTeague as sympathetic bottom dog replaces McTeague as animalistic draft horse.[3]

Norris's own comments on the nonideological purposes

1. For discussion of naturalistic themes, see Donald Pizer, *The Novels of Frank Norris,* pp. 63–79; William B. Dillingham, *Frank Norris: Instinct and Art,* pp. 74–75, 83; Charles C. Walcutt, *American Literary Naturalism: A Divided Stream,* pp. 132–38; and Ernest Marchand, *Frank Norris: A Study,* pp. 56–64.

2. New approaches to *McTeague* include the following: Joseph R. McElrath, Jr., "The Comedy of Frank Norris's *McTeague*"; Louis J. Budd, "Objectivity and Low Seriousness in American Naturalism"; Suzy Bernstein Goldman, "*McTeague*: The Imagistic Network"; and Joseph H. Gardner, "Dickens, Romance, and *McTeague*: A Study in Mutual Interpretation."

3. A recent exception to the revised view emphasizing McTeague's humanity can be seen in James K. Folsom, "The Wheat and the Locomotive: Norris and Naturalistic Esthetics," p. 67.

of fiction are relevant to any reconsideration of his work. In an essay on the desirability of suppressing the novelist's personality, Norris wrote: "After all in fiction the main thing is fiction."[4] Further, a record of his avowed intentions in *McTeague* reflects a pronounced nonideological bent. In a brief statement to the *Philadelphia Book News* in 1899, Norris said of *McTeague* that his "chief object" was to "produce an interesting story—nothing more." A second aim, he went on, was to raise a "protest against and a revolt from the 'decadent,' artificial and morbid 'prose fancies' of latter-day fiction."[5] Too much can be made of such statements, but they do help to correct the earlier overemphasis on didactic naturalism.

As in *Vandover and the Brute*, the most reliable index of rhetoric and meaning in *McTeague* lies in aesthetic documentation. The presence of such material in a novel dealing with lower-depths tenement life may be something of a surprise, since we expect to find this kind of "solidity of specification" in fiction with settings much different from those of *McTeague*, in novels like Henry James's *The Spoils of Poynton* or Edith Wharton's *The House of Mirth*.[6] But the fact is, art is as important to the texture of *McTeague* as it is to any of Norris's novels that deal explicitly with artists. Unlike *Vandover*, however, *McTeague* poses no ambiguities about art and aesthetic experience. In *McTeague*, all art is of the bargain-basement sort, gaudy, tawdry, often commercially produced, and at times approaching the grandeur of *poshlust*.[7] So this novel sets up no standards for evaluating art, nor does it judge the hero in terms of his

4. "Frank Norris' Weekly Letter."

5. Mukhtar Ali Isani, "Frank Norris on the Purpose of *McTeague*," *American Notes & Queries* 10 (1972): 118. Isani reprints a statement by Norris that appeared under the heading: "Aims and Autographs of Authors," *Philadelphia Book News* 17 (May 1899): 486.

6. The term *solidity of specification* is James's; see "The Art of Fiction," p. 14.

7. A definition and marvelous examples of *poshlust* may be found in Vladimir Nabokov, "Poshlust."

failure to make fine distinctions among the fine arts. Instead, McTeague's response to art—it may not be too much to say his love for art—is always a sign of his bedrock humanity and never of demonic possibility, as in *Vandover*. *McTeague* also differs considerably from *Vandover* in that it suggests a better, healthier aesthetic than one based upon man-made art. Against gilded art *McTeague poses an aesthetic of natural space*. In this essential dialectic resides much of the tension and movement of the novel in regard to both setting and action. In an appreciative essay on *McTeague* Kenneth Rexroth has directed us to the center of Norris's accomplishment: "For those who are too sophisticated to be moved by his hero's tragedy, Norris' meticulous stage setting should make the book worthwhile."[8] Thus *gross tonnage*, one critic's disparaging phrase for Norris's compositional effects, may be a successful impressionistic rendering of the feeling aroused by *McTeague*, but it is not an accurate description of the novel's technique.[9] For that, we need something like the word Ellen Moers chose to praise Dreiser's artistry in *Sister Carrie*: *finesse*.[10]

As a venture in using the most unpromising materials, Norris, in *McTeague*, undertook to explore a decidedly low milieu. After all, had not Henry James in *The Bostonians* used a casual aside on dental-parlor decor *to impugn forever* the taste of one of his characters: "Miss Birdseye had only a bare, vulgar room with a hideous flowered carpet (it looked like a dentist's)."[11] Moments of such genteel revulsion occur in *McTeague* too, as in this notorious authorial comment on the hero's mental capacities and tastes:

> This poor crude dentist of Polk Street, stupid, ignorant, vulgar, with his sham education and plebeian tastes, whose

8. Afterword to *McTeague*, p. 343.
9. Warner Berthoff, *The Ferment of Realism: American Literature, 1884–1919*, p. 225.
10. "The Finesse of Dreiser," p. 111.
11. *The Bostonians*, p. 184.

only relaxations were to eat, to drink steam beer, and to play upon his concertina, was living through his first romance, his first idyl.[12]

Nor is this the only instance of pronounced class consciousness. Describing the excessive lengths taken by the "shop girls, the plumbers' apprentices, the small tradespeople and their like" to appear superior to the " 'tough' element," Norris takes a superior tone: "No people have a keener eye for the amenities than those whose social position is not assured" (p. 80).

But fortunately these are exceptions; most of the time the taste of Norris's "plain people" is rendered through descriptive documentation rather than through summary pejorative judgments.[13] His decision to incorporate this level of taste into his novel is one of the most successful uses of popular culture in American fiction in the nineties, easily matching Stephen Crane's skillful dramatization of lowbrow culture in *Maggie, A Girl of the Streets* (1893) and anticipating Dreiser's equally skillful employment of similar materials in *Sister Carrie* (1900). It is also worth noting that Norris's interest in popular culture was shared by his friends and highbrow aesthetes in San Francisco. Despite their middle-

12. Frank Norris, *The Complete Edition of Frank Norris*, 8:24. Hereafter, all citations to *McTeague* are from this edition and will be included in the text.

13. Haughty dismissal of the tastes of the proletariat is a familiar note in the journalism of the period; for example, Arthur McEwen, a contemporary of Norris, had this to say about the plain people: "But the plain people, especially when at play, are not pleasing. They offend taste." ("The Plain People: How They Behave on the Sunday Picnic Boat When At Play"). One of the profound contributions that naturalism made to American literature, Louis Budd has contended, lay in overcoming this kind of strongly disapproving attitude toward the down-and-out: "Naturalism can be described as taking a huge and aggressive stride in compassion toward characters whom novelists had still cheated out of a squarely respectful hearing, such as the illiterate, the stupid, the crudely violent, or the unreflective, and toward characters—the groups were often assumed to merge—of the lowest social classes" ("Objectivity and Low Seriousness in American Naturalism," p. 43).

and upper-middle-class backgrounds, Les Jeunes were as interested in observing popular culture and plebeian taste as in promoting high culture. Gelett Burgess tried his hand at stories dealing with working-class people;[14] Bruce Porter gave Norris the idea for a story about a poor Jewish shopkeeper;[15] and Burgess and Norris delighted in watching "the most varied audience in the whole world"[16] at the Orpheum, the leading vaudeville theater in the city, or at the Mechanics' Fair, where among the "scent of peanuts and popcorn . . . 'Art' wore the aspect of being enormously popular."[17] Indeed, it seems to have been a part of the bohemian style to mingle with the bustling polyglot throngs of the city and to value out-of-the-way cafés where aesthetes and proletarians alike could enjoy themselves free of contamination from the Philistines.[18]

In one respect *McTeague* is a guidebook to plebeian taste, a kind of manual of kitsch art. The quality of taste is mirrored in the cultural activities that McTeague and Trina enjoy during their courtship. On one of their outings they visit the Mechanics' Fair, where Trina expresses her artistic values:

> "Of course," she told the dentist, "I'm no critic, I only know what I like." She knew that she liked the "Ideal Heads," lovely girls with flowing straw-coloured hair and immense, upturned eyes. These always had for title, "Reverie," or "An Idyll," or "Dreams of Love." (p. 170)

14. See, for example, the sketches collected in Joseph M. Backus, ed., *Behind the Scenes: Glimpses of Fin de Siècle San Francisco*, especially "The Red House: A Midnight Colloquy on Happiness in the Latin Quarter," pp. 109–15.

15. Instead of creating a story from Porter's suggestion, Norris used it to illustrate a point in an essay, "Fiction is Selection."

16. Gelett Burgess, *Bayside Bohemia, Fin de Siècle San Francisco and Its Little Magazines*, p. 38.

17. Bruce Porter, "The Beginning of Art in California," p. 30.

18. Porter Garnett, one of Les Jeunes, recalled evenings when he, Norris, Burgess, and others had supper and conversation in the Latin Quarter. Letter to Franklin Walker, 26 March 1931. Franklin Walker Collection, Bancroft Library, Berkeley, Calif. Cited by permission of Director, Bancroft Library.

Such commentary is of course familiar; the "Ideal Heads" remind us of the "Home Book of Art" drawings in *Vandover and the Brute*. In fact this passage, a revision of a Harvard theme, appears in an abbreviated version in *Vandover*, where in chapter 7 Bessie Laguna, Ida Wade's friend, attends the Mechanics' Fair with her boyfriend and voices the same critical theory as Trina.

One of the most famous sections of the novel wonderfully captures the tastes of McTeague and Trina. This is the visit to the Orpheum in chapter 6, a chapter that has not always been appreciated fully because of the attention that has been given to the famous pants-wetting episode and the attendant question of Norris's expert revision of the offensive passage. The Orpheum, "San Francisco's Great Music Hall," was established in 1886 by Gustav Walter and by 1896, according to an ad in its program, was drawing a weekly audience of twenty-five thousand people.[19] It brought together every week an extraordinary variety of acts and "artists," as Norris calls them, thereby separating himself from the possible taint of excessive approval. There is evidence, however, that Norris liked the Orpheum about as much as McTeague and Trina do. He and Burgess did several *Wave* interviews with Orpheum performers, including one by Norris with a Professor Leonidas, who had a cat-and-dog act.[20] Part of the Orpheum's appeal may have derived, as Joseph M. Backus has ingeniously suggested, from elements similar to those that informed the *Lark*. Backus argues that the rapid and illogical juxtaposition of acts and the fluctuations of moods from low comedy to high sentimentality in vaudeville theater are rather like the organizational incongruities and alternation of ballades with cartoons in the *Lark*.[21]

Extant *Orpheum Programmes* suggest that Norris was

19. *The Orpheum Programme*, 28 December 1896.

20. See "A Cat and Dog Life: Leonidas, and His Views upon the Members of His Troupe." For an excellent study of this side of Burgess's and Norris's interests, see Backus, *Behind the Scenes*.

21. *Behind the Scenes*, pp. 30–31.

totally accurate in his presentation of the night's performance in *McTeague*. A week's bill for May 1895, for example, featured the following acts: cornet player; German comedians; "dashing singing soubrette"; Spanish athletes; comedy-sketch artists; "Padewhiskie" (a star attraction, with Will H. Fox in a burlesque of Ignace Paderewski); "Somewhat Different" comedian; California baritone; novelty artists.[22] A June 1896 performance was highlighted by "Edison's Latest Marvel: The Vitascope: The Photo-Electric Sensation of the Day."[23] The acts in *McTeague* are probably a conflation of various performances attended by Norris, but it is of course entirely possible that he simply transcribed one week's show. In any case the variety and types of acts correspond very closely with actual Orpheum bills. Norris describes McTeague, Trina, her mother, and Owgooste excitedly pouring over the program:

> While waiting they studied their programmes. First was an overture by the orchestra, after which came "The Gleasons, in their mirth-moving musical farce, entitled 'McMonnigal's Courtship.'" This was to be followed by "The Lamont Sisters, Winnie and Violet, serio-comiques and skirt dancers." And after this came a great array of other "artists" and "specialty performers," musical wonders, acrobats, lightning artists, ventriloquists, and last of all, "The feature of the evening, the crowning scientific achievement of the nineteenth century, the kinetoscope." (p. 84)

In their responses McTeague and Trina reveal themselves to be the perfect audience for popular culture. After listening to the minstrels "wrestle a tune out of almost anything," McTeague is deeply moved: " 'That's what you call musicians,' he announced gravely. 'Home, Sweet Home,' played upon a trombone. Think of that! Art could go no farther" (pp. 87–88). Trina responds with such delight to the "Society Contralto's" rendition of "sentimental songs" that she "split her new gloves in her enthusiasm" (p. 88).

---

22. *The Orpheum & Entr'Acte Entertainer Programme*, 1, no. 2 (13 May 1895).
23. *Orpheum Programme*, 13 June 1896.

On the way home they review their impressions, and Mc-
Teague sums up the level of their entertainment and appreciation when he recalls fondly "the fellow with the
burnt-cork face who played 'Nearer, My God to Thee' on the
beer bottles" (p. 93). The absolute rightness of everything
that happens in this scene is borne out in an incidental way
by an advertisement in a 1 November 1897 *Orpheum Programme*. The ad, highlighted by a drawing of a big molar,
announced that Van Vroom Electro-Dental Parlors had eight
skilled operators, lady attendants, and German- and French-
speaking dentists. The Orpheum was the perfect objective
correlative of dental-parlor taste.

The aesthetic milieu of *McTeague* serves far more complex purposes than merely providing opportunities for
broad comedy such as is evident in the Orpheum chapter.
The double feat of Norris's achievement is to portray an
age's vulgarity and yet to enlist our respect for the integrity
of the hero's aesthetic response, even though he lives amidst
a world of dreck and of single-minded commercialism. Mc-
Teague's aesthetic integrity is defined by his loyalties and
by his wife's disloyalties. The key aesthetic objects in Mc-
Teague's simple life are itemized in an early passage describing his dental parlors:

> Three chairs, a bargain at the second-hand store, ranged
> themselves against the wall with military precision underneath
> a steel engraving of the court of Lorenzo de' Medici, which
> he had bought because there were a great many figures
> in it for the money. Over the bed-lounge hung a rifle
> manufacturer's advertisement calendar which he never used.
> The other ornaments were a small marble-topped centre
> table covered with back numbers of *The American System
> of Dentistry*, a stone pug dog sitting before the little stove,
> and a thermometer. A stand of shelves occupied one corner,
> filled with the seven volumes of *Allen's Practical Dentist*. On
> the top shelf McTeague kept his concertina and a bag of
> bird seed for the canary. The whole place exhaled a mingled
> odour of bedding, creosote, and ether. (pp. 3–4)

The steel engraving, the pug dog, the concertina, and the
canary are sacred objects to McTeague; they engage his

loyalties, and he gives them up only with great regret. In one of those pivotal acts in the novel that accelerate the downward slide, Trina sells everything in their household in order to keep from drawing on the lottery prize money. A "veritable scene" occurs when she inventories the items to be sold (p. 235), and McTeague is moved to eloquence over the prospect of losing two of his aesthetic possessions:

> "Why," he would cry, "I've had 'em ever since—ever since I *began*; long before I knew you, Trina. That steel engraving I bought in Sacramento one day when it was raining. I saw it in the window of a second-hand store, and a fellow *gave* me that stone pug dog." (p. 235)

He refuses absolutely to yield either the concertina or the canary, and puts a Not for Sale tag on each. Later, after they are living apart, Trina pawns the concertina on which for many years he has played his "six lugubrious airs" (p. 2). This treachery moves McTeague to murderous rage and is an important motivating factor in his killing his wife. The canary, of course, he never relinquishes, carrying it even into Death Valley.[24]

By comparison, Trina's aesthetic possessions are merely things, material manifestations of status, and are charged with less intense emotions and elicit no permanent loyalties. It is true that for her too the week of the sale is a "long agony" (p. 233). The prospect of losing her kitchen utensils makes Trina remember "her raids upon the bargain counters in the house-furnishing departments of the great downtown stores" (p. 234). As the sale goes on, she suffers from such results as seeing her "gay tidies" adorn her friend Miss Baker's chair (p. 240). Even so, it is Trina's decision to sell everything, including their wedding photograph, though Trina's reaction when Mr. Grannis purchases it and returns it to her is ambiguous. She says, "I had forgotten to put it away. Of course it was not for sale" (p. 241). The only object left in the desolate apartment when the sale is over,

24. For a good discussion of the "spiritual" qualities of these objects, see Goldman, "*McTeague*: The Imagistic Network," pp. 95–97.

Trina's wedding bouquet, has been "preserved by some un-known and fearful process" (p. 241). The point is clear. Trina will sell anything; McTeague will not. His attach-ment to aesthetic objects testifies to a humanity that his wife lacks. Thus Trina's statement about her love of the "pretty things" is the shallowest kind of sentimentality: "We've got to leave here—leave this flat where I've been—where *we've* been so happy, and sell all the pretty things; sell the pictures and the melodeon" (p. 227). Their limited artistic activities illustrate the same point. McTeague plays on his concertina for pleasure and self-expression. Trina easily gives up her melodeon and carves her wooden ani-mals only for money.[25]

McTeague's aesthetic integrity is apparent as well in his perception of the single most vulgar object in the novel, the golden tooth. Uniformly interpreted as a symbol of greed and Gilded Age values, the tooth is also an aesthetic entity and is so perceived by McTeague. True, the tooth expresses his ambition and his envy of the more successful dentist who first owns it, and true, in McTeague's eyes it signifies status. But he also thinks of the tooth as "gorgeous" (p. 4) and "wonderful, beautiful" (p. 128). Further, he touches it "as if it were something sacred" (p. 128). At another level the tooth remains emblematic of the age. Made of French gilt, it is a gaudy, crass reminder of the fashion that Edith Wharton and Ogden Codman complained of in 1897: "Today, after

25. My analysis of values symbolized by aesthetic attitudes agrees with the findings of Joseph Gardner, who summarizes the characters' groping expressiveness: "The affirmation of essential humanity strug-gling for existence in a world of dehumanizing force, is the story of McTeague, and the description of the human damage wrought by confusing money with the vital processes of life, is the story of Trina ("Dickens, Romance, and *McTeague*: A Study in Mutual Inter-pretation," p. 81). In a recent Marxist reading of the novel, Lewis Fried argues that "Norris trivializes the outlets such characters have for the instinct of workmanship" and calls McTeague "the picture of the bathetic artist" ("The Golden Brotherhood of *McTeague*," p. 39). Perhaps so, but Norris does not trivialize the emotion nor the qualita-tive difference between McTeague's and Trina's self-expression.

a period of reaction during which all gilding was avoided, it is again unsparingly used, under the mistaken impression that it is one of the chief characteristics of the French styles now once more in demand. The result is a plague of liquid gilding."[26]

Uniformly, taste in *McTeague* with reference to man-made objects is bad. But there is another kind of aesthetic experience that the novel puts forward as superior to conventional aesthetic representation. This is an aesthetic of space, as opposed to an aesthetic of constriction. The first aesthetic is what McTeague gropes toward; the second defines Trina completely. Like *Vandover and the Brute*, *McTeague* is a novel of houses and rooms, but unlike *Vandover* it contains a counterrhythm of space, openness, and natural landscapes. Both tendencies are developed in the courtship of McTeague and Trina. It is out-of-doors where McTeague in fact wins Trina. On picnics and excursions she is drawn to his enormity; only within walls does she find him coarse and unseemly. And McTeague performs much better in the country than in the city. In the park he is able to outwrestle opponents like Marcus Schouler with astonishing ease, whereas in Frenna's saloon he is baffled at Marcus's attack and narrowly escapes serious harm from the hurled knife.

Pastoral assumptions underlie the couple's countryward excursions. Trina, the city girl, captures the essence of the pastoral in her excitement over a picnic: "You take your lunch; you leave the dirty city all day; you race about in the open air, and when lunchtime comes, oh, aren't you hungry? And the woods and the grass smell so fine" (p. 58). The courtship here is something like that of Blix and Condy, but it is continually modified by the realistic facts of the urban landscape. There are no pure escapes to arcadian country in *McTeague*. Thus, one of those wrestling matches turns into an ear-biting, arm-snapping brawl. Also, the landscape that

26. *The Decoration of Houses*, p. 10.

evokes the pastoral repose is anything but arcadian. In one scene McTeague plays the mute swain serenading his lady by a mudbank:

> The wind blew strong, carrying with it the mingled smell of salt, of tar, of dead seaweed, and of bilge. The sky hung low and brown; at long intervals a few drops of rain fell.
> Near the station Trina and McTeague sat on the roadbed of the tracks, at the edge of the mud bank, making the most out of the landscape, enjoying the open air, the salt marshes, and the sight of the distant water. From time to time McTeague played his six mournful airs upon his concertina. (p. 71)

In this terrain, a transitional stage between urban and natural landscapes, McTeague and Trina are "making the most out of the landscape," and McTeague is shaping an aesthetic response upon his concertina. Without Trina, the landscape would be even better, conferring thereby the additional solace of solitude.[27] But the irony of McTeague's final disposition is that in his flight toward space he ends up with the wrong kind; he ends up in Death Valley, which is neither ocean nor fertile land but the bed of "some prehistoric lake" (p. 353).

The expansive rhythm is counterpointed in the courtship by the small constrictive milieu associated with Trina. On a visit to the Sieppe house McTeague finds himself alone in Trina's room:

> It was an ordinary little room. A clean white matting was on the floor; gray paper, spotted with pink and white flowers, covered the walls. In one corner, under a white netting, was a little bed, the woodwork gayly painted with knots of bright flowers. Near it, against the wall, was a black walnut bureau. A work-table with spiral legs stood by the window, which was hung with a green and gold window curtain. Opposite the window the closet door stood ajar, while in

27. The first critic to treat McTeague as a pastoral hero was Richard Chase, *The American Novel and its Tradition*, pp. 198–202. A similar view, with emphasis on native American roots, is found in George W. Johnson, "The Frontier Behind Frank Norris' *McTeague*." Aesthetic documentation corroborates their readings.

the corner across from the bed was a tiny washstand with two clean towels. (p. 67)

The emphasis on smallness and on pretensions toward gentility defines the dimensions of Trina's aesthetic. In such a room, his "lady's bower," McTeague sees himself as an "intruder . . . with his enormous feet, his colossal bones, his crude, brutal gestures" (p. 67). Measuring his size and tastes against hers, he wrongly assumes that Trina is superior: "She was too good for him; too delicate, too refined, too prettily made for him, who was so coarse, so enormous, so stupid" (p. 43). Such evaluations are invariably associated with an indoor setting. As we have seen, McTeague in the park or by the sea is a compelling figure before whom Trina's sensibilities are powerless.

Marriage spells retrenchment, constriction, Trina's smallness.[28] Once the sexual consummation is achieved and marital inertia sets in (*McTeague*, like *Vandover*, is about habit and routine), the question of taste and refinement becomes uppermost in Trina's attitude toward her giant husband. Their life is to be in rooms, not in parks; and, indoors, McTeague is gross and awkward in Trina's eyes. So she sets out to improve his tastes. The changes are surface ones of hygiene and appearance. He begins to dress better, wash more often, be courteous to women, smoke a higher-priced cigar, drink better beer, and read the newspaper. Further, he begins to dream of owning a small house with a "grass plat in front and calla-lilies" (p. 165). At the high point of their financial stability Trina and McTeague consider buying a house, "a wooden two-story arrangement, built by a misguided contractor in a sort of hideous Queen Anne style, all scrolls and meaningless millwork, with a cheap imitation of stained glass in the light over the door" (p. 172). Any of Norris's friends would have recognized

28. On this point George W. Johnson has observed: "McTeague's world is one of expansion, his tastes gross, his requirements quantitative. Trina's experience, on the other hand, is constrictive, her tastes delicate, her standards qualitative." "Frank Norris and Romance," p. 58. This is accurate only with reference to size, not quality.

the accuracy of the attack on Gilded Age architecture in this passage; in fact any of them could have written the same thing, because at one time or another all of Les Jeunes scoffed at the same bad style and inorganic tackiness. This house, which is very similar to the Sieppe home with its "funny red mansard roof of oval slates," represents Trina's most complete domination of McTeague, the usurpation of his aesthetic by hers (p. 66).

Trina's constrictive aesthetic defines McTeague's life from the moment he is ensnared by the mystery of sex until the time when that aesthetic is pushed to its narrowest limits and McTeague makes a stunning Darwinist aesthetic judgment. From that point on, the outward countermovement resumes, climaxing in the desert scenes. The dynamics of constriction versus expansion are noted with barometric exactness in the extensive descriptions of rooms and their furnishings. The married life of the McTeagues begins on the top floor in a lower-middle-class tenement house and ends in a sordid lower-depths apartment on the bottom floor.[29] The first place, decorated by Trina, is an index of her tastes and values:

> Three pictures hung upon the walls. Two were companion pieces. One of these represented a little boy wearing huge spectacles and trying to smoke an enormous pipe. This was called "I'm Grandpa," the title being printed in large black letters; the companion picture was entitled "I'm Grandma," a little girl in cap and "specs," wearing mitts, and knitting. These pictures were hung on either side of the mantelpiece. The other picture was quite an affair, very large and striking. It was a coloured lithograph of two little golden-haired girls in their nightgowns. They were kneeling down and saying their prayers; their eyes—very large and very blue—rolled upward. This picture had for name, "Faith," and was bordered with a red plush mat and a frame of imitation beaten brass.
>
> A door hung with chenille portières—a bargain at two

29. Zola's *L'Assommoir*, most certainly an important literary source for *McTeague*, contains a similar pattern of symbolic dwelling places. It may be that Norris learned more from Zola than a catalog of smells.

dollars and a half—admitted one to the bedroom. The bedroom could boast a carpet, three-ply ingrain, the design being bunches of red and green flowers in yellow baskets on a white ground. The wall-paper was admirable—hundreds and hundreds of tiny Japanese mandarins, all identically alike, helping hundreds of almond-eyed ladies into hundreds of impossible junks, while hundreds of bamboo palms over-shadowed the pair, and hundreds of long-legged storks trailed contemptuously away from the scene. This room was prolific in pictures. Most of them were framed coloured prints from Christmas editions of the London *Graphic* and *Illustrated News*, the subject of each picture inevitably involving very alert fox terriers and very pretty moon-faced little girls. (pp. 136–37)

Such extensive description repays close attention. The Grandma and Grandpa pictures, a fine example of department-store art, express perfectly the infantile, sentimental cast of Trina's mind. They echo a motif developed at length in the meeting and courtship of McTeague and Trina: the adolescent or childlike state of their sexual awareness. They also project an ironic future: McTeague and Trina as grandparents who are never parents (though McTeague begins to dream of a son named Daniel). The third painting, all sentiment and innocence and religiosity crowned with a "frame of imitation beaten brass," derives from those "Ideal Heads" that Trina admired at the Mechanics' Fair. The bedroom wallpaper, with the *hundreds* of tiny Japanese mandarins, further suggests the bad taste that characterizes everything about the place. The concern with numbers is peculiarly Trina's, as is her delight in counting the gold pieces; McTeague's chief concern, of course, is size. The effect of *hundreds* is to convey a crowded, cramping atmosphere, the Lilliputian world of Trina. The prints from the London papers, though probably left there by the former occupant, a photographer, nevertheless fit Trina's overall conception well by repeating the sentimental motif of the innocent girl. The idealized dogs contrast with McTeague's aesthetic dog —the inscrutable stone pug dog—and with two actual dogs: Marcus Schouler's, like its owner a noisy, cowardly sort, and the dog in the water-pump cage at the Sieppe house. All are far removed from the stylized fox terriers. The quality of art in the McTeague household is ruthlessly exposed when the apartment is invaded by strangers during the auction: "Young women—the candy-store girls and florists' apprentices—came to see the fun, walking arm in arm from room to room, making jokes about the pretty lithographs and mimicking the picture of the two little girls saying their prayers" (p. 239).

The McTeagues' second dwelling, a small apartment in the rear of the same tenement building, results from Trina's unwillingness to draw upon her savings when McTeague loses his dental practice. In some respects this single room recalls the decor and atmosphere of Trina's bedroom in her father's house. Only here the effort at genteel prettiness has been dropped; everything is reduced to a grubby functionalism:

> The room was whitewashed. It contained a bed, three cane-seated chairs, and a wooden washstand with its washbowl and pitcher. From its single uncurtained window one looked down into the flat's dirty back yard and upon the roofs of the hovels that bordered the alley in the rear. There was a rag carpet on the floor. In place of a closet some dozen wooden pegs were affixed to the wall over the washstand. There was a smell of cheap soap and of ancient hair-oil in the air. (p. 231)

Perhaps the most revealing detail here is the absence of a closet, a notation that recalls McTeague's plunging himself into Trina's clothes hanging in the closet of the Sieppe house. In the present room there is no evidence of feeling, no sensuous apprehension at all. And with Trina's increasing neglect of minimal household chores, the room grows quite foul. It becomes "grimy" and takes on "an aspect of desolation and cheerlessness lamentable beyond words" (pp. 256–57). It is this degradation, symbolized by the canary's feeble chittering, that leads McTeague to his finest perception in the novel. He tells Trina that she likes living in a "rat hole" (p. 254). Here the Darwinist and aesthetic insights are merged in one compelling image. By naturalism's standards, rats are the lowest of beasts. If McTeague is a bit of a beast himself, he is a gigantic one who, as he is fond of saying, cannot be made small of.

The second dwelling also foreshadows the last McTeague household, a hovel visible from the top floor of the tenement house. In search of cheaper quarters Trina seizes upon the first-story apartment formerly inhabited by Zerkow the miser. This place has a kind of negative grandeur and measures how far the McTeagues have fallen. Consisting of a single room "abominably dirty," it is linked by imagery with two other vistas (p. 285). The bulging wallpaper grotesquely recalls their first apartment, and the "rising muddy tide" of "filth of the alley" ironically echoes their courtship by the sea (p. 286). The room also possesses some aesthetic detritus: the wedding picture (which remains only because Mr. Grannis bought it and returned it to Trina) and the canary.

A third object, the most important, is the golden tooth. What happens to the rooms is paralleled by what happens to the tooth, for Norris carefully notes the tooth's relation to each setting. In its first location, outside McTeague's dental parlors, when everything is happy in his life and marriage, the tooth has curious, transforming effects upon the objects inside. The stone pug dog reflects its light, the canary is stimulated to sing, Lorenzo de' Medici "seemed to ogle the thing out of the corner of one eye," and the colors of the rifle manufacturer's calendar grow dim in comparison with this "greater glory" (p. 129). In the second living quarters the tooth is stored in a corner and gives off a "monstrous, distorted, brilliant" light (p. 245). The only aesthetic object in the room, it is a vivid image of the gigantic figure rendered ludicrous by a constrictive milieu. Like its owner, it needs space for the restoration of aesthetic harmony. In Zerkow's place the tooth reaches its ultimate debasement: "The gigantic golden molar of French gilt, enormous and ungainly, sprawled its branching prongs in one corner of the room, by the footboard of the bed. The

McTeagues had come to use it as a sort of substitute for a table" (p. 286). The words describing the tooth are identical to those applied to McTeague throughout: gigantic, enormous, ungainly, sprawled. Its degradation mirrors his, mirrors the loss of space, the neglect of beauty.

Faced with Trina's indifference to squalor, McTeague begins to search for an alternative landscape. It will have to be out-of-doors, it will have to offer qualities that life in Trina's house does not, it will have to be spacious. The sea is ideal, offering a symbolic opposite of the "rising muddy tide" of trash that invades the apartment. By the sea McTeague is a figure restored to aesthetic dignity:

> He liked the solitude of the tremendous, tumbling ocean;
> the fresh, windy downs; he liked to feel the gusty Trades
> flogging his face, and he would remain for hours watching
> the roll and plunge of the breakers with the silent, unreasoned
> enjoyment of a child. (p. 283)

This seascape recalls of course an earlier scene in McTeague's life, when he was courting Trina beside the mudbank.

Thus is introduced a counterrhythm to the enclosure of rooms, and the novel begins to build toward the last three chapters, the explosion into the desert. From Howells on, this ending has brought objections from critics lamenting its melodrama and its abrupt change of setting. Norris himself insisted to Howells that the ending was appropriate: "I agree in every one of your criticisms always excepting the anti climax, the 'death in the desert' business. I am sure that it has its place."[30] As the Harvard themes show, the ending was not just tacked on, as once thought, but was present in Norris's original conception of the novel.[31] Interestingly, the desert scenes have also drawn praise as a unit without respect to the rest of the novel. Edward Dahlberg,

---

30. Norris to Howells, March 1899(?), *The Letters of Frank Norris*, ed. Franklin Walker, p. 34.

31. See *A Novelist in the Making: A Collection of Student Themes and the Novels Blix and Vandover and the Brute*, ed. James D. Hart, pp. 88–89.

for example, has proclaimed: "Death Valley is what makes Frank Norris."[32] Thematically and structurally the ending of *McTeague* is justified; far from being anticlimactic, it climaxes the evaluation of landscapes, of interior and exterior space, that forms the central and controlling tension of the novel.

The desert chapters contain one description of an interior, the office of the Big Dipper Mining Company. The description is a coda for the rest of the novel. McTeague enters the office to apply for work, "noting the changes that had been made since he had last seen this place":

> There was a telephone on the wall. In one corner he also observed a stack of surveyor's instruments; a big drawing-board straddled on spindle legs across one end of the room, a mechanical drawing of some kind, no doubt the plan of the mine, unrolled upon it; a chromo representing a couple of peasants in a ploughed field (Millet's "Angelus") was nailed unframed upon the wall, and hanging from the same wire nail that secured one of its corners in place were a bullion bag and a cartridge belt with a loaded revolver in the pouch. (p. 325)

The fact that the chromo's title is given in parentheses indicates the care with which Norris records McTeague's consciousness. Millet is outside the experience of McTeague, who recognizes neither the artist nor the cultural context of the painting.[33] But the *Angelus* does a great deal more than reflect McTeague's lowbrowness; it projects a pastoral and traditional world, a peasant culture unavailable to McTeague, a peasant himself. The figures in the painting are a man and a woman, apparently husband and wife, paused in their work, stilled by the sounding of the Angelus bell from a steeple dimly visible in the background. They are emblems of a rude life of toil and reverence. Their society is

32. "Stephen Crane: American Genius," p. 60.
33. *The Angelus* was well known in California, and Millet's *The Man With A Hoe*, which was even more famous, was owned by a San Francisco patroness. "Famous Pictures Owned on the West Coast, II."

stable; the church bell commands their respect and orders their days. The *Angelus*, dramatizing the "time-tested verities of work, companionship, and the guidance of Providence,"[34] has obvious ironic parallels with the lives of the McTeagues, who through the loss of meaningful work, the death of companionship caused by routine and attrition, and the absolute lack of faith in Providence or any external model of belief, have destroyed each other. In the world of McTeague and Trina there is no Angelus, no ploughed field. That is part of their tragedy.

Other details in the Big Dipper Mining Office suggest both its distance from Millet's world and the reasons for this distance. The telephone, a product of an industrial civilization, has penetrated even this primitive mining country. It is one of those machines that symbolize city life and the kind of complexity before which McTeague, who understands neither urban communication nor transportation, is largely helpless. Another symbolic detail is the bullion bag, one of the countless versions of the gold motif in the novel. The central impulse of McTeague's world, whether he is in the city or in Placer County, is to get gold. Significantly, it is not McTeague's central impulse. The third detail is the revolver in the pouch, emblematic of the frontier ethic and one of the echoes of recurring violence in the novel. (Another is the calendar advertising rifles that hung in Mc-Teague's dental parlors.) Telephone, gold, and gun deny the pastoral quietude evoked by the Millet painting.

Outside the mining office lies an alternative landscape, the vast Western spaces that console and nourish McTeague. Wild, primitive, and enormous, this country appeals strongly to him:

> The life pleased the dentist beyond words. The still, colossal mountains took him back again like a returning prodigal, and vaguely, without knowing why, he yielded to their influence—their immensity, their enormous power, crude and blind, reflecting themselves in his own nature, huge, strong, brutal in its simplicity. (p. 329)

34. Amy Lee Turner, "Milton and Millet," p. 227.

Here McTeague experiences the kind of satisfaction that he had found by the sea, away from Trina's single-minded materialism, her rat-hole world.

Yet McTeague is not allowed to remain in this country so commensurate with his size and strength. City forces drive him away. Still, he wards off the threat of city power much better here than he was ever able to in the city. He proves a hard man to capture despite the fact that, carrying the bird cage, he is ridiculously easy to trace. In flight from his home, Placer County, McTeague confronts another man dispossessed of his landscape. The Indian buck Big Jim, whom McTeague mutely encounters at a railroad watering hole, is his double:

> An immense Indian buck, blanketed to the ground, approached McTeague as he stood on the roadbed stretching his legs, and without a word presented to him a filthy, crumpled letter. The letter was to the effect that the buck Big Jim was a good Indian and deserving of charity; the signature was illegible. (p. 333)

Looking back, McTeague sees the Indian as a "forlorn and solitary point of red, lost in the immensity of the surrounding white blur of the desert" (p. 334).[35] McTeague winds up equally lost, in Death Valley, and he is a kind of Indian himself, a primitive with nowhere to live, harried by forces that he cannot understand.

On the run, dime-novel fashion, from the man he does not yet know is his former friend and permanent enemy, Marcus Schouler, McTeague heads for Mexico by way of Death Valley. He enters, literally, a place of descent that parallels the kind of descent measured by the declension of rooms. What McTeague needs, what any pastoral hero needs, is stasis. He had it in his dental parlors before Trina came, he had it with Trina in their first living quarters, and he had it briefly in the resumption of his mining career in Placer

---

35. Johnson has commented perceptively on the Indian figure, connecting him with the vanished frontier and seeing McTeague as a frustrated mountainman-hunter ("The Frontier Behind Frank Norris' *McTeague*," p. 104).

County. But certain incomprehensible factors—sexual attraction, greed (Trina's, not his), the law (and Marcus's
hatred)—intervene each time to disrupt his equipoise. So
McTeague finds himself in Death Valley, a landscape that
completes the evaluation of man and setting begun with the
opening pages of the novel. It is a landscape paradoxically
beautiful and inimical:

> It seemed strange that such barrenness could exhibit this
> radiance of colour, but nothing could have been more beautiful
> than the deep red of the higher bluffs and ridges, seamed
> with purple shadows, standing sharply out against the
> pale-blue whiteness of the horizon. (p. 355)

> It was abominable, this hideous sink of alkali, this bed of some
> primeval lake lying so far below the level of the ocean. The
> great mountains of Placer County had been merely indifferent
> to man; but this awful sink of alkali was openly and
> unreservedly iniquitous and malignant. (p. 360)

The alkali soil is the antithesis of Millet's ploughed ground;
this "primeval lake" is the Darwinian opposite of the restorative ocean where McTeague found solace. Here McTeague
has too much space, space without any human dimension.[36]
The counterforces of constriction and space merge in the
last scene. McTeague slays his captor and is handcuffed
to a dead body in the immensity of the desert.

The novel ends with a synecdochic paragraph:

> McTeague remained stupidly looking around him,
> now at the distant horizon, now at the ground, now at the
> half-dead canary chittering feebly in its little gilt prison.
> (p. 375)

36. Three critics have especially added to our understanding of the
ending. Charles S. Watson traces much of the imagery to Dante's
Inferno, arguing that the novel describes "how passions like greed
produce a hell on earth." ("A Source For The Ending of *McTeague*,"
p. 173). Dillingham proposes that the shift of setting "is a counterpart
to McTeague's personal movement toward bestiality" and points out
the appropriateness of McTeague's song to the ending: "No one to
love, none to caress,/ Left all alone in this world's wilderness"
(*Frank Norris: Instinct and Art*, pp. 138–39). Goldman concentrates
on still another unifying element, a series of image patterns stressing
"a pervasive lack of communication and understanding" ("*McTeague*:
The Imagistic Network," p. 97).

Here McTeague, in a state of perceptual confusion, once again sees without understanding; and the canary, representing his aesthetic and human response to the world, sings weakly in its cage.[37] The cage, we cannot forget, is a gilt prison; and, given all that the novel has told us about the aesthetic milieu, the gilt prison also represents the civilization available to McTeague.

37. The canary's positive qualities have a realistic basis, as Keith S. Sheppard has shown. Miners used songbirds to detect poisonous gases. "A New Note for McTeague's Canary," p. 217.

The Aesthetic Nineties
and the Huge Conglomerate West
of *The Octopus*

Donald Pizer has observed that "a book could be written about the sources of *The Octopus*."[1] His own book on Norris (1966) definitively traces the intellectual influences on Norris's evolutionary theism, and Robert Lundy's dissertation on *McTeague* and *The Octopus* (1956) uncovers many of the economic facts that Norris drew upon, from the Mussel Slough episode to more contemporaneous economic conditions in San Francisco in the 1890s. The discussion to follow explores still another considerable body of sources and influences: Norris's substantial and precise knowledge of the artistic ambience of San Francisco during the formative years of his own artistic development.

The Octopus reflects Norris's rediscovery of the California he had known and his encounter with a California far more protean than the one he had viewed primarily as an urban field for fiction.[2] To create this culminating response to the aesthetic nineties and to his San Francisco associates, to capture this West of city and country, Bohemian Club and barn dance, Norris spent several months in San Francisco and the San Joaquin Valley gathering facts and impressions.[3] Thus, more so even than *McTeague*, *The Octopus* was a researched novel. Norris's return to San Francisco in 1899 must have produced some remarkable moments of déjà vu. The *Lark*, for example, was brought to his attention again when Gelett Burgess gave him an inscribed two-volume set. Also, one wonders about his visits to the Mechanics' Library to in-

1. *The Novels of Frank Norris*, p. 121.
2. Before *McTeague* was published, Norris wrote Isaac F. Marcosson: "The novel of California must now be a novel of city life" ([December 1898], *The Letters of Frank Norris*, ed. Franklin Walker, p. 23).
3. In a letter to Marcosson (13 September 1900) Norris exclaimed about the time he had put in on *The Octopus*: "It is the hardest work I ever have done in my life, a solid year of writing and 4 months preparation—bar two months" (*Letters*, p. 67).

vestigate a past that he had known so well. Did he find there or in his own papers or in his memory the name *Swanhilda*, which he used for the ship on which Presley is bound for India at the novel's end? In any case Norris reported on a ship named *Swanhilda* in a *Wave* article of 1897.[4] Newspaper clippings that survived among his papers further testify to Norris's mosaicist reliance on actuality. Both the slaughter of the sheep at the beginning and S. Behrman's death at the end had their origins in newspaper stories of the day: "Oakland Train Hits Sheep Band: 75 Die" and "Sinks To Death In A Grain Pit: Two Workers Fall Into Great Vat And One Is Taken Out Dead."[5]

Out of this welter of personal experience and researched fact, Norris telescopes the artistic nineties—and over twenty years of economic struggle—into one fin-de-siècle moment. The spiritual date of the book might be said to be 1899; its actual key moments of history are 1880, 1894, 1897, and 1899. The first represents, of course, the well-known Mussel Slough incident, which, as part of the background of the novel, has received much enlightened comment.[6] The second date is that of the California Midwinter International Exposition, a fair inspired by the famous Columbian Exposition at Chicago in 1893; the third represents *Wave* articles on wheat harvesting, winegrowing, and relief ships, to cite some particular pieces that contain direct analogues in the novel; the last is the year in which Edwin Markham's "The Man With the Hoe" appeared.

In tracing the aesthetic data of *The Octopus*, I hope I am not engaging purely in source study. Although interesting in its own right, aesthetic documentation in this novel serves to clarify the portrait of the central character, the poet Presley; to illuminate Norris's ideas about the relationship between various modes of art and nature; and to reveal

4. "Hunting Human Game: How Watch and Wait is Kept for the 'Swanhilda.' "

5. Frank Norris Collection, Bancroft Library, Berkeley, Calif. Cited by permission of Director, Bancroft Library.

6. See, for example, Irving McKee, "Notable Memorials to Mussel Slough."

still another structural pattern that binds together the relationships among the three young men of the novel, Presley, Vanamee, and Annixter, and reveals their essential connection with the philosophical "answer" of the novel's conclusion: the much-debated optimistic ending. To plunge into the clusters of data surrounding the education of the poet Presley is to risk losing proportion. Certainly I do not mean to imply that the aesthetic material supersedes in importance or magnitude the larger thematic patterns of economic struggle and of man's philosophical status in the natural world, the big themes of *The Octopus*. But aesthetic commentary there is in plenty, and one would do well, in a comprehensive reading of the novel, not to ignore it.

Presley's education begins in the opening chapter and is still continuing at the novel's close. Though the fortunes of many characters are traced, principally those of three intellectual young men, as Kenneth Lynn has observed,[7] Presley is the most important single character, which is not to say that he is the most memorable. Annixter is probably that; certainly he was to such contemporary readers as Jack London.[8] But it is Presley whom we see the most of; he is both a sympathetic link between disparate characters and an actor in, or an observer of, most of the major events of the novel. Jack London identified Presley as Norris, but he is not, at least in any positive sense.[9] Later critics are closer to the mark when they call Presley an "anti-Norris"[10] or say that in creating Presley, Norris was "shriving himself of one aspect of his own personality."[11] What Norris was in fact doing was projecting a composite artist of the nineties, a complex fusion of influences. Presley is an amalgam of aesthetic

7. Introduction to *The Octopus*, pp. v–xxv.
8. "The Octopus," in *Jack London: American Rebel*, ed. Philip Foner, p. 509.
9. Ibid.
10. *The Literary Criticism of Frank Norris*, ed. Donald Pizer, p. 101.
11. Richard Chase, *The American Novel and Its Tradition*, pp. 195–96. Warren French makes the important point that *The Octopus* is an exercise in point of view. *Frank Norris*, p. 92.

images: Mallarmean faun, San Francisco aesthete, socialist poet in the Markham tradition, and would-be natural poet.

The connection between Presley and Mallarmé is doubt-less the most surprising item in this list. The basis for such a claim lies in the closing pages of the first chapter. The scene is the climax of the hero's meditations upon a usable subject for the poetic imagination. A postgraduate of an Eastern university who is living among the wheat ranchers in the San Joaquin Valley, Presley has spent the day rambling about the countryside, talking to acquaintances, and thinking fret-fully of possible themes for a long work. Drawn from both past and present, these themes include the colorful, legen-dary Spanish period of California history; the story of Vanamee's loss of his sweetheart and his flight into the romantic wastes of the Southwest; the mission world of Father Sarria, and the primitive, adventurous aspects of rais-ing wheat on a titanic scale. Late in the afternoon he goes to a solitary place and inventories the real and imagined ex-periences of the day. Both in general movement and in specific parallels, Presley's experience is a recasting of Mallarmé's "L'Après-midi d'un faune: églogue" (1876). Mallarmé's poem explores the conflicting claims of the imagined and the real. It opens with the persona, a faun, announcing his intent to recall and make permanent an exquisite experience, a day's dalliance with two nymphs of surpassing loveliness. But the faun, it turns out, is not certain that the nymphs ever existed; he may have only dreamed them. After repeated efforts to recreate the mood and flavor of that sensuous delight, the faun by the end of the poem seems contented with the unresolvable ambiguity of his experience and gives himself to sleep.

The passage introducing Presley's reverie is crucial; it invokes by allusion Mallarmé's poem:

> Presley climbed to the summit of one of the hills—the highest—that rose out of the cañon, from the crest of which he could see for thirty, fifty, sixty miles down the valley, and, filling his pipe, smoked lazily for upwards of an hour, his head empty of thought, allowing himself to succumb

to a pleasant, gentle inanition, a little drowsy, comfortable in his place, prone upon the ground, warmed just enough by such sunlight as filtered through the live-oaks, soothed by the good tobacco and the prolonged murmur of the spring and creek. By degrees, the sense of his own personality became blunted, the little wheels and cogs of thought moved slower and slower; consciousness dwindled to a point, the animal in him stretched itself, purring. A delightful numbness invaded his mind and his body. He was not asleep, he was not awake, stupefied merely, lapsing back to the state of the faun, the satyr.[12]

In general terms, the poem and the scene follow the same pattern: a half-conscious, dreamy, sensuous reverie is succeeded by euphoric attempts to reimagine a vanished or incompletely realized experience, which are then followed by a return to ordinary consciousness. Both works dramatize the claims of the real and the fanciful upon the imagination; both explore twilight areas of consciousness. The parallels extend, however, beyond this similarity of design and theme. First, both fauns are artists. Mallarmé employs the conventional pastoral device of reeds to symbolize the faun's creative powers: the memory of the departed nymphs can be approximated only through the agency of art, by piping on the reeds. Norris alludes to Homer to represent the aspirations of his potential artist. Upon emerging from the faun-like dream, Presley reads excitedly from *The Odyssey* and believes that he is at last in possession of his own great poem. The faun's reeds and Presley's worn copy of Homer are thus related symbols.

Second, the settings are quite similar. Mallarmé's faun awakens in a pastoral landscape and creates his vision against a vista of space and golden verdure. Norris's faun, atop a lofty hill, conjures the forms of his poem against the immense golden reaches of the San Joaquin Valley.

A third parallel is the contrast between present experi-

12. Frank Norris, *The Complete Edition of Frank Norris*, 1:41–42. *The Octopus* is contained in volumes 1 and 2. Hereafter, all citations to the novel are from this edition and will be included in the text.

ence and an ancient time. Mallarmé's faun imagines himself thus:

> Alors m'evéillerai-je à la ferveur première,
> Droit et seul, sous un flot antique de lumière,
> Lys! et l'un de vous tous pour l'ingénuite.[13]

In Norris the ancient time is given a specifically European cast. As Presley heads home, his mind a tumult of images, he hears the "*de Profundis*, a note of the Old World; of the ancient régime, an echo from the hillsides of mediaeval Europe, sounding there in this new land, unfamiliar and strange at this end-of-the-century time" (1: 45–46). The language is strikingly close to J.-K. Huysmans's description of the *de Profundis* hymn in *A Rebours*: "Comme une curiosite de l'antique Eglise, l'ame du moyen âge."[14] This observation, which occurs just seven pages after a discussion of Mallarmé and the quotation of three lines from "L'Après-midi," suggests that Norris may have discovered, or renewed his acquaintance with, Mallarmé's work through *A Rebours*.[15] There is no direct evidence, however, to show that Norris knew either Mallarmé or Huysmans. Neither his personal collection, nor his library record at Harvard, nor his critical writings reveal any references to either of them.[16] Yet Norris's knowledge of French literature was based upon firsthand acquaintance with the language and upon courses he took at both Berkeley and Harvard. Lars Ahnebrink, without much evidence at all, supposed that Norris knew *A Rebours*.[17] The first chapter of *The Octopus* suggests that he knew Mallarmé or Huysmans or both.

There is, finally, an obvious generic similarity between the two works. Mallarmé's poem is by designation an ec-

---

13. *Poésies*, p. 67.

14. *Oeuvres Completes de J.-K. Huysmans*, 7:307.

15. Ibid., pp. 296–300.

16. Lars Ahnebrink, *The Beginnings of Naturalism in American Fiction*, pp. 460–62; Willard E. Martin, Jr., "Frank Norris's Reading at Harvard College."

17. *The Beginnings of Naturalism in American Fiction*, pp. 309–14.

logue, and many of the traditional elements of the form are present in the poem: the objective pastoral setting, the use of soliloquy and dialogue, and the emphasis on mood and theme rather than on character and action. Norris's scene depends upon the same features: a pastoral landscape; the figure of the goat-poet engaged in a subjective dialogue; the mood and the tonal qualities predominating, until just before the end, over the expected novelistic concern with character and action. Mallarmé's eclogue ends quite differently from Norris's. Unable to sustain the image of the nymphs, the faun lets the dream go, subsiding into sleep, where he will confront only the absolute emptiness of their former reality.[18] His reverie, one might say, is emptied of content. Norris's eclogue has, instead, a more volatile ending: the reverie is charged with a new and ominous content. The contrast with the beginning of the eclogue, with Presley's reverie and his excited flights of inspiration, could hardly be more extreme as Norris brings Presley down from the shepherd's hill to witness the massacre of those pastoral clichés, lambs and sheep. We are also reminded of Annixter's advice to Presley when he encouraged him to "look at that herd of sheep as you go up . . . You might write a poem about 'em. Lamb—ram; sheep graze—sunny days. Catch on?" (1:27). Presley's conception of "terrible, formless shapes, vague figures, gigantic, monstrous, distorted" (1:44), which so stimulates his epic imagination, is now grimly realized in the bulk and the destructive force of the roaring locomotive. The train runs athwart Presley's pastoral interlude and destroys the landscape's "sense of peace, of security, and placid contentment" (1:47). The eclogue, that quiet form, is exploded by the intervention of an unharmonized force.

The episode of Presley's reverie has implications for the novel as a whole. It is the first symbolic definition of the figure of the artist, a key theme throughout the work. Characteristically, in this initial venture of the imagination,

18. Throughout these remarks I am indebted to Wallace Fowlie's analysis in *Mallarmé*, p. 152.

The cover drawing from book 1 of the bound edition of the *Lark*.

Presley fails. He cannot reconcile the diffuse elements of landscape, memory, Homer, and prosaic reality—ranch workers, trains—with the "beauty of his poem, its idyl" (1:46). Later in the novel Presley's long poem, "The Toilers" —his attempted epic and a great popular success—is satirically exposed by an unfavorable comparison with the painting that inspired it. Presley's aesthetic fails because, as we shall see, it is too derivative and because its impetus does not come from nature.

It also seems likely that another source for the faun image was the cover drawing of book 1 of the bound edition of the *Lark*. Entitled "Faun Piping" and drawn by Bruce Porter, the figure was exactly that, a faun playing on pipes. To Norris it must have typified everything that he disliked about the *Lark*'s literary assumptions: its phony classicism and its reverence for studio art insulated from the real life of the city and the wheat ranches.

The faun-artist figure is but one of a series of topical references in the novel to actual artists in San Francisco in the 1890s. When the novel opens, Presley is in revolt against his background, against his training in literature at an Eastern university and, more particularly, his former artistic activities in San Francisco. Norris's concreteness in satirizing Presley's San Francisco connections should not surprise us, nor should the fact that the organ under attack is the *Lark*. Although this critique is often subterranean, the principal targets are discernible. Details broadcast throughout the novel, when seen together, reveal a design, a covert and carefully managed criticism of the *Lark*'s aesthetic and of genteel art in San Francisco.

In the first chapter of book 2 Norris pauses from the principal narrative action, the struggle between the wheat ranchers and the railroad, to sketch the artistic atmosphere of San Francisco. The sketch focuses upon Mrs. Cedarquist's salon, a collection of artists and performers that includes a Russian countess, an aesthete, a Muhammadan widow, a Klondike poet, a Japanese youth, a Christian Scientist, a Cherokee folksinger, a university professor, and others.

an interesting catalogue

Their common denominator is phoniness, and there is no mistaking Norris's opinion:

> It was the Fake, the eternal, irrepressible Sham; glib, nimble, ubiquitous, tricked out in all the paraphernalia of imposture, an endless defile of charlatans that passed interminably before the gaze of the city, marshalled by "lady presidents," exploited by clubs of women, by literary societies, reading circles, and culture organizations.[19] (2:29–30)

Certain figures satirized in the Cedarquist catalog are based on real artists and intellectuals of Norris's acquaintance. The easiest to identify is the Japanese poet whose verse Norris quotes:

> The Japanese youth, in the silk robes of the *Samurai* two-sworded nobles, read from his own works—"The flat-bordered earth, nailed down at night, rusting under the darkness," "The brave, upright rains that came down like errands from iron-bodied yore-time." (2:29)

Though these lines might appear to be the invention of a satirist, they are in fact the work of a *Lark* poet, Yone Noguchi (1875–1947). The first quotation is the opening line of "The Invisible Night"; the second, the opening line of "The Brave Upright Rains." Both poems were originally published in number 15 of the *Lark* (July 1896). "The Invisible Night" is thoroughly representative of Noguchi's early poetry:

> The flat-boarded earth, nailed down at night
> rusting under the darkness. The Universe
> grows smaller, palpitating against its destiny.
> My chilly soul,—center of the world, gives
> seat to audible tears,—the songs of the cricket.
> I drink the darkness of a corner of the Universe,
> —Alas! square, immovable world to me, on my bed!
> Sugesting what—god or demon?—far down, under
> my body.

19. Norris's widow spoke of his intense dislike for literary clubs and cults and of his "great scorn for the small literary person." Interview with Franklin Walker, 16 May 1930. Franklin Walker Collection, Bancroft Library, Berkeley, Calif. Used by permission of the Director, Bancroft Library.

> I am as a lost wind among the countless atoms of
> high Heaven!
> Would the invisible Night might shake off her
> radiant light, answering the knocking of my soft-
> formed voice!

Norris has misquoted one word, *flat-bordered* for Noguchi's *flat-boarded*. In quoting from the second poem he departed a bit more from the original, writing "The brave, upright rains that came down like errands from iron-bodied yore-time" for "The brave upright rains come right down like errands from iron-bodied yoretime." In both instances, though, one feels that Norris had the poems before him or else remembered them very accurately indeed. The satire is withering, and twice Norris comments directly on Noguchi's poetry, calling them "the most astonishing poems, vague, unrhymed, unmetrical lucubrations, incoherent, bizarre" (2:28) and "the inarticulate wanderings of the Japanese" (2:30). Another contemporary local observer took as harsh a stand on Noguchi's work as Norris did. A reviewer for the *Call* said that Noguchi's poems were "more vague than jellyfish" and placed the poet in the baleful company of Max Nordau's degenerates: "One can imagine the zest with which Nordau would have classified the author of this. Among the ranks of his 'degenerate' how he would have hurled his choicest adjectives, hysterical, egomaniacal at his defense-less head."[20]

In attacking Noguchi, Norris was also criticizing his old friends Gelett Burgess and Porter Garnett, both of whom had played a large role in introducing the aspiring Japanese poet to the world. In his introduction to Noguchi's maiden appearance in the *Lark*, Burgess took partial credit for the composition of the poems and championed their appeal. He felt that their strangeness of both form and idea was their best quality:

> An exile from his native land, a stranger in a new civili-
> zation,—a mystic by temperament, race, and religion,—

20. [untitled review, under page heading "Books and Bookmakers," by W. Kelley] *San Francisco Call*, 24 January 1897, p. 23.

these lines which I have rephrased, setting his own words in a more intelligible order, are his attempts to voice the indefinable thoughts that came to him on many lonely nights; the journal of his soul,—nocturnes set to words of a half-learned foreign tongue; in form vague as his vague dreams.[21]

Garnett also had a hand in Noguchi's early efforts, as he stated in a letter to the *San Francisco Call* in 1896 defending Noguchi against charges of plagiarism:

My claims to a hearing in the matter are fourfold: to-wit, as a friend of Mr. Noguchi, as a collaborator with Gelett Burgess in the editing and publishing of Mr. Noguchi's poems, as a devout admirer of Poe upon whose poems the charges are based, and as a contemner of plagiarism and plagiarists.[22]

Years later, Garnett described his and Burgess's efforts as paraphrases and cited "The Brave Upright Rains" as an example of one poem that he had helped Noguchi with.[23] Garnett and Burgess stuck by Noguchi during the plagiarism attack and proved their loyalty by publishing his first book of poems, *Seen and Unseen, or Monologues of A Homeless Snail*, in 1896.[24]

Although Noguchi had his detractors, he had some illustrious supporters as well. Carolyn Wells, a *Lark* sympathizer and its only woman contributor, wrote a laudatory letter-review to the *Critic* in 1896, quoting in their entirety the two poems that Norris indicts in *The Octopus*.[25] Willa Cather, familiar with Noguchi's first two volumes, *Seen and Unseen* (1896) and *The Voice of the Valley* (1897), made a summary estimate in a review for the *Courier* in

21. "The Night Reveries of an Exile."
22. "Yone Noguchi, the Japanese Poet, is Defended from a Charge of Plagiarism," *San Francisco Call*, 29 November 1896, p. 21.
23. "Yone Noguchi," *Nation* 113 (7 December 1921): 666–67.
24. For additional commentary on the Noguchi plagiarism row, see D. B. Graham, "Yone Noguchi's 'Poe Mania,'" and Joseph M. Backus, "Gelett Burgess: A Biography of the Man Who Wrote 'The Purple Cow,'" pp. 231–33. Backus's study also contains a discussion of Noguchi's presence in *The Octopus* (pp. 166–67).
25. "The Latest Thing in Poets."

1898: "While Noguchi is by no means a great poet in the large, complicated modern sense of the word, he has more true inspiration, more melody from within than many a greater man."[26] Noguchi's fame grew so large that Burgess became envious,[27] and it is entirely possible that one of the pieces in Burgess's most outré journalistic effort, *Le Petit Journal des Refusees*, was a satirical parody of Noguchi's obscurantist style. In this ultimate little magazine, which Burgess described as a "rollicking, whooping gabble of ultra-nonsensical verbiage."[28] and for which the premise was that all work included had been rejected by other magazines, one of Les Jeunes wrote "The Ghost of a Flea," the first few lines of which are:

> There was an astonishing oval blue moon a-bubble among
> the clouds, striking a sidewise chord of wild, blatant
> reluctance athwart the bowl of curds with which I stroked her.
> (Oh, Love! dead, and your adjectives still in you!)[29]

Noguchi's least successful poems are never far from the level of this parody.

Norris could scarcely have avoided knowing about Noguchi and his work, for during the years 1896 to 1900 Noguchi lived in a cabin owned by Joaquin Miller in the hills above Oakland.[30] In the 1897 Christmas issue of the *Wave* a poem by Noguchi entitled "Love" appeared on the same page as Norris's "Little Drama of the Curbstone: A Merry Christmas."[31] Also, there is one personal reference to Noguchi in Norris's correspondence, though from the context

26. "Two Poets: Yone Noguchi and Bliss Carman," 2:579.

27. Backus, "Gelett Burgess," p. 194.

28. *Bayside Bohemia, Fin de Siècle San Francisco and Its Little Magazines*, p. 26.

29. *Le Petit Journal des Refusees*, no. 1 (1 July 1896), n.p. The *Wave* called *Le Petit Journal* a "mad little ebullition of gilded wallpaper and distorted human limbs and Gelett Burgess" and wished that "so much imagination and wit" could be "harnessed to some neat, modern, and not too flashy vehicle." [untitled] *Wave* 15 (25 July 1896): 9.

30. For an interesting account of Noguchi's life, see his autobiography, *The Story of Yone Noguchi*.

31. *Wave* 16 (25 December 1897): 7.

it is impossible to tell whether Norris actually knew Noguchi. From New York, Norris wrote Charles Warren Stoddard
in 1900: "What ever became of Yone Noguchi. He never
showed up here at this office that I ever heard of there is
little that I can do for him I know, but mebbee that little
would help. I take it though that he is not in extremities."[32]

Both Noguchi's poetry and his posing must have bothered
Norris a good deal for him to have included so transparent
a portrait of a friend of Les Jeunes in his novel. He also
included other local figures, but because less information is
available, these may be identified only tentatively. Joaquin
Miller, Noguchi's patron and the most flamboyantly colorful artist in the bay area, was possibly the model for Norris's
description of one poet: "The bearded poet, perspiring in
furs and boots of reindeer skin, declaimed verses of his own
composition about the wild life of the Alaskan mining
camps" (2:29). Miller affected a variety of Western styles,
including bearskin capes, bowie knives, and a particularly
outlandish Spanish concoction featuring high-heel boots,
red or yellow shirts, scarves, and a sombrero.[33] Julian Hawthorne has left a memorable picture of Miller's dress and
an explanation of two of its purposes:

> Joaquin, a licensed libertine, charming, amiable, and harmless,
> amusing the Club and himself by costuming his part as
> Poet of the Sierras; sombrero, red shirt open at the neck,
> flowing scarf and sack, trousers tucked into spurred boots,
> long hair down over his shoulders, and a great blond beard.
> "It helps sell the poems, boys!" he would say, "and it tickles
> the duchesses."[34]

Jack London, as well, seems a distant possibility to have
served as a model, since an *Overland* article carried a photo-

32. *Letters*, p. 68.
33. Robert W. Ditzler, "Bohemianism in San Francisco At The
Turn of the Century," p. 42. See also M. M. Marberry, *Splendid
Poseur: Joaquin Miller—American Poet* (New York: Thomas Y. Crow-
ell Co., 1953), p. 232. Marberry claims that Norris was a "steady
guest" at Miller's house (p. 201); this seems to be without founda-
tion, however.
34. *Shapes That Pass: Memories of Old Days*, p. 78.

graph of "Jack London in Arctic Costume" in 1900.[35] Most interestingly, Gelett Burgess sported costumes on occasion too. He showed up for a party honoring the *Lark* in 1897 "bedecked in strange skins and crimson robes and purple things."[36]

The rather sleazy intellectual pretentiousness of literary and artistic coteries in general was a subject that had held Norris's satirical attention for years. Although the intellectuals in the Cedarquist catalog cannot be identified, there are hints from Norris's *Wave* days as to the kind of behavior that angered him. "The 'Bombardment,' " a satirical piece of 1897 written under one of Norris's pseudonyms, Julian Sturgis, described the process by which one became a litterateur. A young society man visits Crete the day after a bombardment, writes an account of it, and is then invited by one ladies' group after another to read his paper. He attends "mauve" teas and is "lorgnetted without mercy."[37] Later he reads the paper at a scientific gathering:

> I read it next at the Geographical Society, sandwiched in between Dr. Harkness' "Paleolithic Theories" and David Starr Jordan on "Retrograde Movements of the Common Arab." I was the only one who didn't have lantern-slides, and the audience of six women and two men filled the Academy of Sciences with their yawns.[38]

Norris's clever thrust at David Starr Jordan, president of Stanford University, suggests that anonymity was one reason for the Julian Sturgis pseudonym. Professors such as Jordan were perhaps the model for the professor in the Cedarquist catalog. Similarly, Mrs. Cedarquist was apparently modeled on a woman who ran on about Norris's "power" when his mother introduced her son at a literary meeting in 1899.[39] In "The 'Bombardment' " Norris cap-

35. Ninetta Eames, "Jack London," *Overland Monthly* 35 (May 1900): 419.

36. "Gelett Burgess in Odd Skins."

37. "The 'Bombardment': How a San Francisco Essayist Made a Little Go a Long Way."

38. Ibid.

39. Franklin Walker, *Frank Norris: A Biography*, p. 251.

tured the very type in "Mrs. Beebe," a "woman of gush and giggle."[40]

The thing that connected all such artists, intellectuals, and patrons in Norris's mind was a reliance on appearance rather than on substance. Norris's contempt for aesthetic fraudulence had always been strong; by 1901 it was an *idée fixe*. In *The Octopus* he compares these fakirs to "shell-game tricksters" at a county fair (2:30). In a 1901 essay he pinpointed the basic element of pretense:

> For the one idea of the fakir—the copyist—and of the public which for the moment listens to him, is Clothes, Clothes, Clothes, first, last and always Clothes. Not Clothes only in the sense of doublet and gown, but Clothes of speech, Clothes of manner, Clothes of custom. Hear them expatiate over the fashion of wearing a cuff, over a trick of speech, over the architecture of a house, the archeology of armour, and the like.[41]

Norris was hardly alone in the period in his dislike for phony artists and intellectuals. The *Wave* warned against such people repeatedly. In 1897, upon the failure of a local arts and crafts guild, of which Willis Polk was a leading member, the *Wave* attacked those responsible for its failure: "There is, it would seem, a place for such an institution in San Francisco if the poseurs who like to fasten themselves like a blister on anything that promises advertising, can be squelched."[42] In 1899 the *Wave* cautioned San Francisco citizens to be on the alert for "A. A. Advani, a Hindoo prince—of fakirs."[43]

Among the Cedarquist circle the chief figure is Hartrath, a painter for whom Norris and his poet-protagonist Presley feel total scorn. Presley meets Hartrath at a men's club, probably the Bohemian Club, San Francisco's most fashionable private club in the nineties. Its members were composed of artists, businessmen, and politicians, and some of

40. "The 'Bombardment': How a San Francisco Essayist Made a Little go a Long Way."
41. "The True Reward of the Novelist."
42. "Things and People," *Wave* 16 (30 January 1897): 7.
43. "Things and People," *Wave* 20 (9 December 1899): 9.

that first group were Norris, Peixotto, Burgess, Keith, Garnett, and Charles Rollo Peters.[44] Significantly, it is ladies' day when the Derricks and Presley are introduced to Hartrath, who is described in the most unflattering terms: "A certain middle-aged man, flamboyantly dressed, who wore his hair long, who was afflicted with sore eyes, and the collar of whose velvet coat was sprinkled with dandruff" (2:15). This is the type that Norris warned against in essay after essay, advising the American writer to seek no contact with the "hothouse artist" and to remain "far from the studios and the aesthetes, the velvet jackets and the uncut hair, far from the sexless creatures who cultivate their little art of writing as the fancier cultivates his orchid."[45] The studio artist is either sexless or homosexual; Hartrath seems to be the latter when he says in response to Mrs. Cedarquist's praise of his picture: " 'I am a mere bungler. You don't mean quite that, I am sure. I am *too* sensitive. It is my cross. Beauty,' he closed his sore eyes with a little expression of pain, 'beauty unmans me' " (2:31–32). A surviving page of the holograph contains a more extensive indication of mock self-criticism and disgusting weakness on Hartrath's part:

> In the face of an exquisite landscape I became also [sic] helpless with emotion to such a point that my head trembles, my breast refuses to obey my will I cannot paint what I feel. The faults in my little painting are due to that. I am too sensitive. I am one constant quiver of sensibilities. A harsh criticism hurts me like a blow. I am a little child.[46]

In the characterization of Hartrath, Norris was of course doing little more than bringing a popular stereotype of the artist into his novel. When a local journalist pictured what the authors of the *Lark* might look like, he had the same

44. The activities of several of these members are recorded in Clay M. Greene, ed., *The Annals of the Bohemian Club*, vol. 3.

45. "Novelists of the Future: The Training They Need," p. 14.

46. Leaf 190, holograph, Frank Norris Collection. Quoted by permission of Director, Bancroft Library.

stereotype at hand: "I have not the pleasure of knowing Bruce Porter and Gelett Burgess, the editors of this Beardsleyesque publication, but I am quite sure that they give afternoon teas and talk with a beautiful 'lithp.' "[47] Similarly, a writer who wanted to portray Ernest Peixotto favorably used the stereotype as a negative comparison; Peixotto was "not of the wild, hare-brained order of Bohemians, not of the far-off, gazing-into-the-infinite kind; not the unkempt, long-haired fellow."[48]

But Norris also invests Hartrath with a particularity that vivifies his fraudulence. The central attraction at the club and the ladies' chief object of admiration is a painting by Hartrath that is being raffled off for the Million-Dollar Fair, or what Mr. Cedarquist calls the Gingerbread Fair. This painting, described in detail, provides another submerged link with the *Lark* aesthetic. It is a conventional pastoral scene of the kind much in vogue in California in the 1890s:

> But the focus of the assembly was the little space before Hartrath's painting. It was called A Study of the Contra Costa Foothills, and was set in a frame of natural redwood, the bark still adhering. It was conspicuously displayed on an easel at the right of the entrance to the main room of the club, and was very large. In the foreground, and to the left, under the shade of a live-oak, stood a couple of reddish cows, knee-deep in a patch of yellow poppies, while in the right-hand corner, to balance the composition, was placed a girl in a pink dress and white sunbonnet, in which the shadows were indicated by broad dashes of pale blue paint. (2:26)

Whether Norris had a particular painter in mind is impossible to tell, but it seems clear that a popular regional style was his object. The young society women who view the painting offer a clue when they invoke Daubigny, Millet, and Corot by way of praise. The Barbizon school was the favorite model for California regionalists of the 1890s, and the lead-

47. *Arthur McEwen's Newsletter*, undated clipping [probably 1895], Gelett Burgess Collection, Bancroft Library. Cited by permission of Director, Bancroft Library.

48. Peter Robinson, "Peixotto and his Work," p. 133.

ing painter of the day, William Keith, had definite affinities with this school.[49] Charles Keeler traced the beginning of this influence to the Loan Exhibition of 1891: "The work of Corot, Daubigny, Rousseau and the other landscape artists of their group interested him very deeply and he profited by his study of their characteristics."[50] Norris also mentioned the Barbizon element in Keith's work in remarks on the 1896 Winter Exhibition: "This artist is always admirable, still clinging to the precepts of the school of D'Aubigny and Corot, delighting in sombre greens and blacks and bitumens, painting pictures that are full of sharp contrasts, broad and sketchy and vigorous."[51]

The *Lark* prized Keith's work and in one issue reproduced one of his paintings alongside works by Millet and Corot.[52] It is possible, but not likely, that Norris may have intended Hartrath's painting to satirize Keith directly. There are tangential facts to indicate that this might have been the case. Keith's work was displayed at the Bohemian Club in 1897, as Norris noted in a *Wave* review.[53] Also, Keith drew the frontispiece for Yone Noguchi's second volume, *The Voice of the Valley*. Finally, certain elements in the Hartrath painting, the oaks and the maiden, were staples in Keith's work. What seems more likely, however, given the generally fa-

49. The *Wave* ranked Keith with Corot early in the decade: "Keith has in his studio several of the greatest landscapes he has ever painted. . . . They are works of genius, as good as Corot" ("Splashes," *Wave* 8 [6 February 1892]: 7). Evidence of Keith's prominence is abundant. Charles Keeler spoke for a host of critics when he observed in 1906: "Of local painters William Keith stands alone in his art as a master of landscape" (*San Francisco and Thereabout*, p. 47).

50. "Friends Bearing Torches: A Company of Great-Hearted Californians," p. 32. Quoted by permission of Director, Bancroft Library.

51. [Note on the Winter 1896 Exhibition at the Hopkins House].

52. *Lark* 2, no. 19 (November 1896): n.p. Backus has made the extremely interesting suggestion that the color reference to cows in Hartrath's painting is a satirical ploy aimed at Burgess's most famous contribution to the *Lark*, the "Purple Cow" quatrain ("Gelett Burgess," pp. 166–67).

53. "Pictures To Burn: A Slim and Dreary Art Exhibition at the Hopkins House."

vorable comments on Keith that dot Norris's art criticism, is that the target of attack was Keith's genre, or what we might call live-oak regionalism. Gibes at the popularity of such landscapes crop up often in the period. Thus an 1895 *Wave* article complained of "a lot of portraits and some still-life paintings and the inevitable 1893 or 1891 or 1892 or 1890 or other 1800 of the Hill-Yosemite cases."[54] But the widespread acceptance of the Barbizon landscape style dominated the scene. Landscapes by Corot, Daubigny, Courbet, Dupre, and Keith were rated the best work on display at the Midwinter Fair in 1894.[55]

The extent to which live-oak regionalism was negotiable currency in the nineties is borne out by an amusing incident recounted in the *San Francisco Call* in 1896. One Jules Mersfelder, who claimed to paint in the "quality school" and who said that Keith was working "in the same direction," spent a month in the hills, where he produced several canvases bearing such titles as *A Foggy Morning in the Oaks* and *Sunset*. These he promptly sold to a store that regularly handled Keith's work; when Keith discovered them he was furious, but Mersfelder had already skipped town.[56]

Throughout the satirical attack on Mrs. Cedarquist's salon, and on Hartrath especially, Norris is equally interested

54. Scarabeus, "Spring Art." One observer took pride in the wide-spread adherence to landscape painting: "In the coming exhibition the whole State has been covered" ("Some Gems of Art Painted for the Fall Exhibition").

55. Leslie Martin, "Paintings at the Midwinter Fair." Testimony to the impact of Millet, Corot, Courbet, and Daubigny at the 1891 Loan Exhibition was eloquent. Wrote the *Wave* reviewer: "One's first impulse on entering the rooms of the exhibition is to seek out Millet's 'Man With the Hoe,' and standing before such a canvas one can forget the sentimental gush that has almost made the name of Millet a by-word" and "After standing and taking in one of the simple and soberly complete works of Corot, Courbet, or Daubigny, one can hardly understand how one ever could have admired, nay, even looked at, one of the many tricky, over-crowded canvases which so often fill our exhibitions and abuse dame nature" (A.F.M., "Art Loan Exhibit").

56. "Paintings like Keith's."

in the audience that applauds bad art and thereby contributes to its existence. Hartrath's painting elicits a volley of critical clichés:

> The ladies and young girls examined the production with little murmurs of admiration, hazarding remembered phrases, searching for the exact balance between generous praise and critical discrimination, expressing their opinions in the mild technicalities of the Art Books and painting classes. They spoke of atmospheric effects, of middle distance, of "*chiarooscuro*," of fore-shortening, of the decomposition of light, of the subordination of individuality to fidelity of interpretation. (2:26–27)

The women conclude "that the reddish-brown cows in the picture were reminiscent of Daubigny, and that the handling of the masses was altogether Millet, but that the general effect was *not quite* Corot" (2:27). By 1891 Corot and Daubigny were already something of clichés in San Francisco art circles. A *Wave* article gave advice on how to respond to paintings at the Loan Exhibition:

> Approach every painting with an air of "I would know my child among a thousand." Exclaim "Ah! here we have our Daubigny, or Diaz, or Corot," as the case may be, as if a long standing intimacy with the works of the artist has made you perfectly familiar with his individuality. Consult your catalogue surreptitiously.[57]

The society women overrate Hartrath's derivative regionalism; as products of genteel art schools, they lack contact with the proper source of evaluation, nature. Nowhere is this clearer than in Mrs. Cedarquist's praise of Hartrath's painting and Presley's sonnet. She gushes, "You two have much in common. I can see so much that is alike in your modes of interpreting nature. In Mr. Presley's sonnet, 'The Better Part,' there is the same note as in your picture, the same

---

57. Harriet Lane Levy, "Art Critics' Guide." Norris made fun of the same kind of schooled ignorance in a review: "The only Young Person that goes to the Art Association reception is the female Art Student, or Art School Girl, as she is sometimes called—an unique creation, whose tongue is trained to the terminology of picture-craft" ("Pictures to Burn").

sincerity of tone, the same subtlety of touch, the same *nuances*—ah" (2:31).

Presley's sonnet, which appeared in print sometime before he left San Francisco for the San Joaquin Valley, was published in a little magazine. This fact, plus the apparent lofty idealism implied by the title, accounts for Presley's detestation of the magazines that he sees lying on Mrs. Derrick's center table at Los Muertos Ranch: "the little toy magazines, full of the flaccid banalities of the 'Minor Poets' " (1:57). Further, Mrs. Derrick, an exponent of polite Eastern gentility and of orthodox literary values, is alarmed at Presley's vehemence: "His savage abuse and open ridicule of the neatly phrased rondeaux and sestinas and chansonettes of the little magazines was to her mind a wanton and uncalled-for cruelty" (1:58). The reason Presley so abhors these magazines is that he is in revolt against them, having earlier been a participant in such cultist and irrelevant activity. In fact, Mrs. Cedarquist thinks of him as a "minor poet" and has been scanning the little magazines looking for more of his work (2:31). It is not farfetched at all to imagine the *Lark* among those magazines beloved by Mrs. Derrick and Mrs. Cedarquist. In Burgess's words, it "ran the gamut of French forms of verse."[58] The link between such magazines and Hartrath is explicit: they have "flaccid banalities" (1:57); he has "flaccid" hands (2:31). Hartrath is an apparition of Presley's former self, a reminder of everything Presley now seeks to avoid.

The aspects of *Lark*-ish art satirized in *The Octopus* are not those humorous qualities that endeared the magazine to readers who turned the "Purple Cow" quatrain into a national byword, but rather the serious, romantic strains that, as Burgess recalled, moved the *Lark* "away from pure nonsense."[59] In 1897, when the *Lark* was over, one of Les Jeunes, probably Burgess, maintained that it was Noguchi's poetry that "gave a new direction to the serious verse the 'Lark' had been publishing, by a series of original poetical

58. *Bayside Bohemia*, p. 21.
59. Ibid., p. 25.

monologues."[60] Apparently this serious side of the *Lark*
struck Norris with more force in 1899 than in 1897, when he
had spoken of the magazine as merely "delightful fooling."
But early in the *Lark*'s career such nonhumorous efforts as
"Rondel of Perfect Friendship" and "Chant-Royal of Romance That Is Not Dead" could be found among the light
essays and cartoons. There were also such forays into romantic apologia as Bruce Porter's prose-poem "Hail To
Thee, Blithe Spirit," which contained sentiments that Norris
could have accepted, except that they were expressed in a
rhetoric he could not accept:

> Art must come out of the earth, and the earth be plowed and
> sowed and reaped by a steady race, before there comes the
> harvest of conscious beauty. And why should we hurry to
> the end of the feast—the tidbit, the *dolce*? Ah! my milkman
> has not! Here he comes at last, with a leap like a bird's to
> duty. Over-measure to every empty can this morning, I'll
> warrant, with a drop on the curb for the cat! God! I'd rather
> pull the teats of a cow than squeeze tubes of cobalt and
> carmine! Let us get out into the air—run wild over the
> Presidio, and then a dash in the bay! Life is a bigger thing
> than art![61]

The principal assumptions maintained here are very similar
to those that Presley discovers during his sojourn in the
San Joaquin Valley: the identification of art with the earth,
the preference for country over city, the embracing of action
in nature.[62] They are also of course quite similar to Norris's
own assumptions, and Porter's last sentence is almost identical to Norris's oft-repeated "life is more important than
literature."[63] But there is something more than faintly absurd about Porter's exclamation. The artist he imagines is

60. A. Jeune, "An End To The Lark: The Brief History of a Freak
Among Freaks," *Wave* 16 (10 April 1897): 8.

61. *Lark* 1, no. 1 (May 1895): n.p.

62. Robert Ditzler has also commented on the "realistic implications" of Porter's passage and its echo of Norris's views; see
"Bohemianism in San Francisco at the Turn of the Century," p. 98.

63. "Why Women Should Write the Best Novels: And Why They
Don't."

still indubitably a studio aesthete dashing about the bay area. The nature that needs to be confronted, and that Presley does eventually confront, is primordial, quite unlike the spurious wildness sought by Porter's artist, which is a pseudopastoral landscape of rhetorical cows.

One of Norris's purposes in spending so much time on art in this chapter—and at various points elsewhere in the novel—is to examine the role and function of the artist in a society impelled by economic energies. The meaning of the aesthetic activity mirrored in the ladies'-day scene is thus a question of considerable importance. The Cedarquists, who hold opposite views, express perfectly the polar images of San Francisco in the nineties. To Mrs. Cedarquist, a patroness and lover of art, San Francisco is indeed a center of culture:

> She spent her days in one quiver of excitement and jubilation. She was "in the movement." The people of the city were awakening to a Realization of the Beautiful, to a sense of the higher needs of life. This was Art, this was Literature, this was Culture and Refinement. The Renaissance had appeared in the West. (2:31)

Seen against a decade of debate on the state of culture in San Francisco, Mrs. Cedarquist's view sounds very familiar, and certainly it is no more inflated than actual opinions expressed in the period. Here, for example, is a visionary flight by Willis Polk, a notable architect who was one of the *Lark* contributors and the sternest of the architectural critics: "When the ages have lent it [California] dignity, it will go down to history with Egypt, with Greece, with Rome and with France. It will be the heritor of all their greatness, but the projector of its own."[64] This was in 1899. Or consider another of the *Lark*'s writers, Bruce Porter, discoursing in 1897 upon the possibilities for high culture in San Francisco: "The time should come when California will be to the United States what Italy was to Europe, and when San

---

64. "San Francisco Beautiful."

Francisco will be to California what Florence was to Italy—a home of a new school of art and architecture."[65]

Reading through the journalism of the period, one can find almost-weekly announcements of the imminent arrival of the renaissance. One can also find the opposite viewpoint, that the hope for a renaissance is ill-conceived or doomed. It was this gloomier view that Norris expressed in his assessments of the local cultural boomlet. In 1897, for example, he satirized the emergence of literary societies and their championing of every trivial literary production by native talent. Asked to read a travel essay about the bombardment of Crete, Norris writes:

> I have been offered a six months' subscription to the 'Overland' for its publication in that magazine, but I know a good thing when I have it, and there are yet clubs in town. For we have begun the revival of culture in San Francisco and have already promised to become a 'centre.'[66]

Looking backward at the end of the decade, Gelett Burgess offered a similar evaluation: "We were badly prepared, both in money and in brains, for the effort to revive California's literary renown, or to create a 'centre.' "[67]

Norris's viewpoint is expressed in the novel by Mrs. Cedarquist's husband, who scoffs at her enthusiasms and sees San Francisco in an entirely different light. To him the city is a "Midway Plaisance" and the state "a paradise of fakirs" (2:19). The first label derives from the Columbian Exposition and San Francisco's own California Midwinter International Exposition of 1894. To understand the importance of Mr. Cedarquist's use of the phrase *Midway Plaisance*, it is necessary to know a little about the context. For Willis Polk explicitly and for Norris symbolically, nothing in the decade so reflected the glaring disparity between na-

65. "The Native Son Monument," *Wave* 16 (11 September 1897): 9.

66. "The 'Bombardment': How a San Francisco Essayist Made a Little Go a Long Way."

67. "Essays in Enthusiastic Journalism. III. 'Phyllida; or, The Milkmaid,' " p. 291.

ture and artifice, possibility and failure, as the Midwinter
Fair. Conceived to promote California's bountifulness and
its mild winter climate, the fair was an architectural disaster,
a gauche mishmash of incongruous styles and cultures.[68]
For the rest of the decade, Willis Polk cited the fair as a
model of unplanned building, arguing in 1896 that it "was
not built at all";[69] and in 1900, commenting on similar mis-
management in the designs for Golden Gate Park, he recalled the fair as his most reliable bad model: "It is a
'midway plaisance,' with its ridiculous collection of lodges,
pavilions, bridges, etc."[70] For Norris, the "Midway Plaisance" image held rich associations of frivolous activity,
trivial amusement, meaningless pleasure. In 1896, when he
visited the Italian-Swiss Colony Vineyard at Asti, north of
San Francisco, he employed the phrase didactically to contrast with the real, the valuable:

> There is nothing Midway-Plaisance about Asti. That's what
> makes it so interesting. There is no artificiality about it, no
> pose. The colonists do not care whether you are interested
> and amused or not. There's no effort at imitation. It's the
> true thing, it's real life, it's business and bread and butter
> and all that.[71]

Here is the formulation that he would proclaim again and
again: real authentic life versus artificiality, posing, and
phoniness.

The Cedarquist debate ends with the Cedarquists in ironic
juxtaposition. The wife has just won Hartrath's painting in
the raffle; and her husband, looking at the "gayly dressed
throng of beautiful women and debonair young men," says
again, "not a city, Presley, not a city, but a Midway Plai-

68. For discussion of the Midwinter Fair, see Joseph Armstrong
Baird, Jr., *Time's Wondrous Changes: San Francisco Architecture,
1776–1915*, p. 41; and Gunther Barth, "California Midwinter International Exposition," n.p.
69. "The University Competition: A Critique."
70. "How To Beautify San Francisco."
71. "Italy in California: The Vineyards of the Italian Swiss Colony
at Asti."

sance" (2:38). One critic, a contemporary of Norris and like him a writer of fiction, was so taken with the city's gaiety and beautiful women that he completely misread this scene. Citing Mr. Cedarquist's statement, Bailey Millard embraced the image: "Here beauty reigned, and everybody who was anybody turned out to see it. Truly in those good old days San Francisco was not a city but a Midway Plaisance."[72] That Norris did not hold such a sanguine view of San Francisco culture is clear. In one passage he summed up his response to the conception of the city as a European-like center. From Lyman Derrick's office window and from his point of view as a man of affairs, we are given an overview of San Francisco:

> It was a continuous interest in small things, a people ever willing to be amused at trifles, refusing to consider serious matters—good-natured, allowing themselves to be imposed upon, taking life easily—generous, companionable, enthusiastic; living, as it were, from day to day, in a place where the luxuries of life were had without effort; in a city that offered to consideration the restlessness of a New York without its earnestness; the serenity of a Naples without its languor; the romance of a Seville without its picturesquesness. (2:3)

Such an analysis tallies closely with Norris's view of the city expressed earlier, in the *Wave* in 1897, and indicates again that many of Norris's attitudes toward culture that are incorporated into *The Octopus* were already formed by 1896–1897. At that time, he expatiated on San Francisco's lotus-land qualities:

> Life in this city of ours is like a little glasslet of liqueur—pungent, sweet, beady, but without foundation, without stability—an appetizer that creates only small desires, easily gratified, and we are content with those.[73]

Evidence in *The Octopus* clinches which side of the cultural debate Norris argued for; to borrow the polar images of the

72. "San Francisco in Fiction," p. 597.
73. "The Opinions of Leander: 'Holdeth Forth Upon Our Boys and the Ways of Them.'"

period, Norris saw San Francisco as closer to a "jay town"[74] than to a "Pallas Athena of the Modern World."[75]

One of the strongest points in Mr. Cedarquist's criticism is its economic implications. The name of the fair in the novel—the Million-Dollar Fair and Flower Festival—underlines this theme. Mr. Cedarquist rails against such activity: "We don't want fairs. We want active furnaces. We don't want public statues, and fountains, and park extensions, and gingerbread *fêtes*. We want business enterprise" (2:18). As Norris's notebook reveals and as Robert Lundy has discussed in detail, Cedarquist's speech is based on a newspaper article on the closing of Pacific Rolling Mills, a two-million-dollar factory.[76] Another article in the notebook, an editorial by John T. Flynn, criticized San Francisco in terms very close to those used by Cedarquist: "It runs to flowers and festal boards, instead of commerce."[77] Cedarquist deplores spending a million to attract Eastern visitors while losing a million because of the closing of his iron foundry. He denounces Hartrath, the fair's cheerleader, to his face and calls the whole thing a "sham of tinsel and pasteboard" (2:19). Hartrath, too, is well aware of the economic underpinnings of the fair. He brags about the money pouring in and tries to influence Lyman Derrick to "further the pretensions of a sculptor friend of his, who wished to be Art Director of the affair" (2:17). But the most damaging indictment of Hartrath and the fair is saved until the very end of the novel. Just before boarding the *Swanhilda* for India, Presley hears an update of the fair's progress from Cedarquist:

> "You know the 'Million Dollar Fair' was formally opened yesterday. There is," he added with a wink, "a Midway Pleasance [*sic*] in connection with the thing. Mrs. Cedarquist and our friend Hartrath 'got up a subscription' to construct a figure of California—heroic size—out of dried

74. Scarabeus, "Spring Art."
75. Elodie Hogan, "Hills and Corners of San Francisco," p. 63.
76. "The Making of *McTeague* and *The Octopus*," pp. 214–15.
77. "Notes. I." Quoted by permission of Director, Bancroft Library.

apricots. I assure you," he remarked with prodigious gravity, "it is a real work of art and quite a 'feature' of the Fair." (2:357)

Hartrath's sculpture, ludicrous to the point of caricature, is actually no more absurd than the kinds of displays on view at both the Columbian Exposition and the Midwinter Fair. At Chicago, for example, California exhibits included five Keith paintings, a "Bean Pagoda of Ventura," "a mighty Liberty Bell, made of oranges and modelled after the old cracked bell of '76," and "two tons of bottled olive oil built high into a new Cleopatra's Needle."[78] The Midwinter Fair contained similar sculptures. A dried-fruit model of the new capitol at Sacramento "clearly reflected the progressive spirit of California today."[79] And Santa Clara County's exhibit, "modeled from materials unknown to the sculptor's art," was a prune sculpture of a horse and rider.[80] Hartrath's dried-apricot creation, it turns out, is as derivatively bad as his study of the Contra Costa foothills. This last word about Hartrath's silliness confirms Presley's opinion. Earlier he had pointed out to Mrs. Cedarquist that Shelgrim, the head of the railroad and a man she idealizes as a Lorenzo de' Medici, supports the fair because it is profitable to do so.

Chapter 1 of book 2, which has necessitated such a long commentary, is crucial in understanding Norris's definitive assessment of the culture that he had known intimately during his formative years. It is also crucial in seeing Presley's predicament. Because he does not participate in the Million-Dollar Fair and because he does not resume his former aesthetic ties with the little magazines, it might be assumed that he can therefore become a successful artist. And indeed, under the influence of Vanamee and the vitalizing contact with the elemental reality of human struggle and of raising wheat, he is moved to produce something superior to his

78. Charles Edwin Markham, "California at the World's Fair."
79. Will A. Marlow, *California Sketches*, pp. 134–35.
80. The *"Monarch" Souvenir of Sunset City and Sunset Scenes. Being Views of California Midwinter Fair and Famous Scenes in the Golden State*, n.p.

earlier efforts, a socialistic poem called "The Toilers." But the immediate stimulus hearkens back to Presley's earlier aesthetic credo, for the poem's source of inspiration is not only nature but also a painting. Shelgrim, the railroad magnate, points out that the painting, which hangs in the Cedarquist home, is superior to the poem.[81] Shelgrim's credentials as an art critic parallel those of the figure on whom he was modeled, Collis P. Huntington, one of the railroad magnates in California known as the Big Four. Huntington owned paintings by Corot and Daubigny[82] and in 1900 donated a Keith painting to the Art Association.[83]

Presley's poem and its connection with a great painting have always been thought to be a fictionalization of the circumstances surrounding Edwin Markham's publication of his famous "The Man With the Hoe" in the *San Francisco Examiner* on 15 January 1899.[84] There is additional evidence to establish further links between Presley's work and Markham's. Presley's title, "The Toilers," was quite possibly taken from an introductory essay that Markham wrote for the Doubleday edition of *The Man With the Hoe* in 1900. *Toiler* is a frequent epithet in this essay: "The Hoeman is the symbol of betrayed humanity, the Toiler ground down through ages of oppression, through ages of social injustice."[85] Other circumstantial facts are of some interest. Presley's poem is "printed . . . in Gothic type, with a scare-

81. Millet's *The Man With the Hoe*, on which Markham's poem was based, was owned by Mrs. Will H. Crocker. See "Famous Pictures Owned on the West Coast, II."

82. John O'Hara Cosgrave, "An Impression of Collis P. Huntington."

83. "Another Gift From Collis P. Huntington: Keith's 'Summit of the Sierras,' Presented to the Art Association." Lundy, who has done much valuable work on the backgrounds of *The Octopus*, seems quite in error, however, when he says that "Huntington was accused of many things in his day but never of possessing 'vast sympathies' or artistic taste" (p. 259). But architectural taste was another matter, if Willis Polk's view is accurate: "Mr. Huntington's views on architecture would shame a Digger Indian." Quoted in Oscar Lewis, *The Big Four*, p. 219.

84. Walker, *Frank Norris*, pp. 261–62.

85. *The Man With The Hoe*, With Notes by the Author, p. 23.

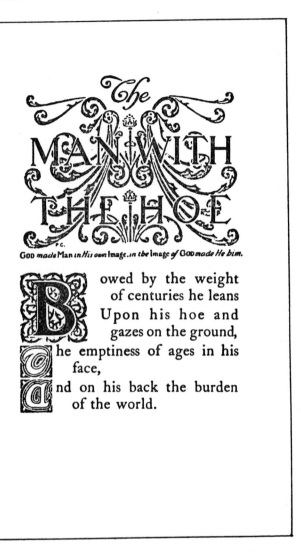

First page from William Doxey's edition of *The Man With the Hoe.*

head title so decorative as to be almost illegible, and . . . [is] illustrated by one of the paper's staff artists in a most impressive fashion" (2:108). This description seems to be an exaggeration of the actual appearance of Markham's poem in the *Examiner*, but Norris may have had in mind another and much fancier printing of the poem. Shortly after the poem's newspaper debut, William Doxey, publisher of the *Lark*, brought out a book edition with illustrations by Porter Garnett. This volume, a very fine piece of fin-de-siècle printing, contained red-and-black-ink scrollwork, numerous miniatures of sections of Millet's painting *The Man with the Hoe*, and a photographic reproduction of the entire painting. It also bore the *Lark* emblem, a faun piping, on the title page.[86] However handsome, this book was a bit of aestheticism that signaled the complete acceptance of the "radical" poem in genteel circles. The same thing happens to Presley's poem. After it has been acclaimed throughout the nation, he visits Mrs. Gerard, the wealthiest person in the novel. She calls him *"notre jeune Lamartine"* and tells him of her and Mrs. Cedarquist's movement to ship grain to the starving people in India (2:315).

In exploring the possible roots of Presley's characterization as a poet, we should not overlook some possible autobiographical influences. Norris, it will be recalled, began his writing career as a poet, with the publication of the chilvaric romance *Yvernelle* in 1891. Partially financed by his mother, the volume was a handsome piece of bookmaking, replete with white and gold binding and illustrations with illuminated figures. Norris was to spend the rest of his authorial career repudiating such aesthetic flourishes. Another possible connection between Presley's poetry and Norris's can be surmised from the kind of verse that Norris wrote. "Crepusculum," published in the *Overland Monthly* in 1892, sounds very similar to what we must imagine Presley's "The Better Part" to have been, a conventional rhetorical

86. *The Man With The Hoe.*

Page from William Doxey's edition of *The Man With the Hoe,* with illustrations by Porter Garnett.

celebration of optimism. The closing lines of "Crepusculum" are enough to give the flavor:

Our Life's a night through which we blindly grope
With outstretched palms, hoping 'gainst falling hope.
Death ushers in the dawn of Life's true day;
Though gray the eve, so is the morning gray.
Be thou uplift, O Heart! Death's visage wan
Is lighted not with twilight but with dawn.

Presley's associations with Mallarmean aestheticism, *Lark* studio art, and Markham's social protests are all pejorative to one degree or another. The only aesthetic mode with which he attempts to align himself that is not criticized is what we might call natural art. This is a mode, however, that Norris is unable to present in convincing terms. The problem is two-fold and has its roots, apparently, in Norris's basic distrust of poets and aestheticism. Both Presley, who would like to be a natural artist, and Vanamee, who by fiat is one, bear telltale signs of opprobrious aesthetic connotations.

In the first place, Presley is never capable of achieving the status of the natural artist, because Norris limits his capacities from the start. For one thing, Presley is a poet, a calling that Norris presents in less than totally favorable terms. The poetic vocation is qualified in such passages as this one comparing Vanamee and Presley: "The one a poet by nature [Vanamee], the other by training [Presley], both out of tune with their world, dreamers, introspective, morbid, lost and unfamiliar at that end-of-the-century time" (1:210). Not only is Presley a poet, he is a poet by training, a status inferior to that of Vanamee, a "poet by instinct" (1:33). Moreover, being a poet precludes wide intellectual ability. The introductory sketch of Presley brings out this deficiency: "His temperament was that of the poet; when he told himself he had been thinking, he deceived himself. He had, on such occasions, been only brooding" (1:6–7). Presley's intellectual efforts confirm this judgment. Attempting to understand the socioeconomic facts of the struggle between the ranchers and the railroad, Presley abandons his favorite poets—Milton, Tennyson, Browning, Homer—for writers like Mill, Malthus, Young, Pushkin, Henry George, and Schopenhauer. All that results, however, is "a confused jumble of conflicting notions" (2:23). "Sick, with over-effort, raging against injustice and oppression, and with not one sane suggestion as to remedy or redress," Presley is indeed not much of a thinker (2:23). There is also something unsettling about his appearance: "Presley with his dark face, delicate mouth, and sensitive, loose lips, in corduroys and laced boots, smoking cigarettes—an interesting figure, suggestive of a mixed origin, morbid, excitable, melancholy, brooding upon things that had no names" (1:203). This sketch links Presley with a number of suspect values: foreignness, effeminacy, hybridism. It suggests a studio artist, a Hartrath without dandruff. Presley's essential aloofness from the common people, despite all his intellectual efforts to differentiate himself from the elitist studio artists, remains a permanent part of his being. His speech to the people at the Opera House, following the bloody battle between the ranchers and the law officers, fails precisely because of its studied literary character: "He had talked as he would have written; for all his scorn of literature, he had been literary" (2:262).

Presley's choice of genre is another indication of his limited perception. He decides that his projected "Song of the West" must be an epic, but only after Vanamee points out to him that the epic form fits Presley's vision of the West as a land of primitive people engaged in a heroic venture. Even so, the epic poem is not the proper genre. A late essay by Norris (1902) consigns the long poem to the past: "There is no doubt the novel will in time 'go out' of popular favor as irrevocably as the long poem has gone out and for the reason that it is no longer the right mode of expression."[87] The essay makes clear what the right mode is:

To-day is the day of the novel. In no other day and by no other vehicle is contemporaneous life so adequately expressed;

87. "The Responsibilities Of The Novelist."

and the critics of the twenty-second century, reviewing our times, striving to reconstruct our civilization, will look not to the painters, nor to the architects nor dramatists, but to the novelists to find our idiosyncrasy.[88]

"The Toilers," in short, ought to be a novel instead of a poem. The *Wave* advanced a similar position in 1894, celebrating the supremacy of the novel and arguing that "the world is tired of the poetic form of expression."[89]

Presley comes to Los Muertos to attempt to find a new basis for art, to make contact with a natural source of experience and inspiration. He tells Vanamee: "It is the man who is lacking, the poet; we have been educated away from it all. We are out of touch. We are out of tune" (1:38). One of Norris's late short stories, "Dying Fires," provides a helpful gloss on Presley's situation, for it approaches the same problem from another direction: the hero, Overbeck, tries to reestablish contact with nature after having written a successful novel and having been lionized in the salons of New York. Overbeck begins as a Presley type; he is educated at a fancy college (in the West, however) where for his commencement exercise he reads a paper on Dante's philosophy. After thus paying homage to genteel culture, he fortuitously returns to the country of his childhood, where "strenuous, eager life, a little primal even yet" still exists.[90] Here in Placer County (McTeague's frontier) Overbeck writes a novel, *The Vision of Bunt McBride*. (Norris published several late stories about a Western "rough" named Bunt McBride.) The book is more a product of environmental influences than of any genius possessed by its author. Summoned East, Overbeck dons his cutaway coat and piqué cravat and is sucked into a literary circle called the "New Bohemians." This group values preciosity, elegant style, abstractions, European avant-gardism, spirituality, and catho-

88. Ibid.
89. "The Decline of Poetry."
90. *The Complete Edition of Frank Norris*, 4:114. Hereafter, all citations to "Dying Fires" are from this edition and will be included in the text.

licity, all the deadly sins for the American writer. Their tastes are broadly satirized:

> Did a sonnet called, perhaps, "A Cryptogram is Stella's Soul" appear in a current issue, they fell on it with eager eyes, learned it by heart, and recited lines of it aloud; the conceit of the lover translating the cipher by the key of love was welcomed with transports of delight. (p. 119)

Under the New Bohemians' tutelage Overbeck learns the language of genteel criticism—tones and philistinisms and allegory and split infinitives (why he did not learn this effete stuff in college we are not told)—and produces a new novel called *Renunciations*. Its landscape is urban, refined, and lifeless; its characters are members of the leisure class. The cultural moths who influenced Overbeck to produce such a novel have by now, though, gone on to a new fad, a "symbolist versifier who wrote over the pseudonym of de la Houssaye" (p. 126). Too late, Overbeck returns to the West, but the fire of creativity "had been stamped out beneath the feet of minor and dilettante poets" (p. 127).

The conflicting claims between East and West, city and country, Europe and America, primitivism and civilization, art and life are laid bare in "Dying Fires." One passage presents the opposing forces as idealism versus realism: "Ah, the spiritual was the great thing. We were here to make the world brighter and better for having lived in it. The passions of a waitress in a railway eating house—how sordid the subject. Dear boy, look for the soul, strive to rise up to higher planes!" (p. 122). The relevance of "Dying Fires" to Presley's condition is clear. The false values of the New York literary cultists—idealism, spirituality, refinement, soft optimism—are the snares from which Presley tries to escape. And Overbeck's virtues—regionalism, sincerity, vitality, honesty—are what Presley is searching for. With Presley the question comes down to Homer versus "The Better Part."

Presley's stay at Los Muertos is not solely a plunge into Homeric primitivism. The presence of Mrs. Derrick and the culture she represents are a vivid reminder of Presley's former training and provide a helpful antithesis for his developing aesthetic. Educated at a young ladies' seminary and capable of teaching literature, music, and penmanship, Mrs. Derrick is a torchbearer of high culture: "Her one ambition was to see Italy and the Bay of Naples. The Marble Faun, Raphael's Madonnas, and Il Trovatore were her beau ideals of literature and art. She dreamed of Italy, Rome, Naples, and the world's great 'art-centres'" (1:55–56). Separated from the cultural possibilities of the city, she finds sustenance in books. Her favorite works are, from Presley's (and Norris's) viewpoint, an index of overrefined, escapist art:

> Her taste was of the delicacy of point lace. She knew her Austin Dobson by heart. She read poems, essays, the ideas of the seminary at Marysville persisting in her mind. *Marius the Epicurean, The Essays of Elia, Sesame and Lilies, The Stones of Venice,* and the little toy magazines. (1:57)

Presley shocks her because he has no use for any of these writers or, excepting his "few chosen deities," for literature either (1:58).

Norris's criticism is full of passages attacking those he conceived of as cultist writers. In one late essay (1901) he defined classic authors as "those gentlemen whose books are bought but not read," and listed these examples: Stephen Phillips, George Moore, Austin Dobson, and Walter Pater.[91] Norris also does not spare the audience of such literature. In another late essay (1902) he relegates elitist assumptions to the past and champions the vulgar relevance of the present-day novel to a newspaper-reading audience:

> Times were different then. One shut one's self in the study; one wore a velvet coat; one read a great deal and quoted Latin; one knew the classics; one kept apart from the vulgar profane and never, never, never read the newspapers. But for the novelist of the next fifty years of this twentieth century these methods, these habits, this conception of literature

91. "The Remaining Seven of Frank Norris' 'Weekly Letters,'" ed. Richard Allan Davison, p. 64.

as a cult, as a refinement to be kept inviolate from the shoulderings and elbowings of the Common People . . . is false, misleading and pernicious.[92]

Such a view is identical to Vanamee's advice to Presley to publish "The Toilers" in the daily press:

> "Your inspiration has come *from* the People. Then let it go straight *to* the People— not the literary readers of the monthly periodicals, the rich, who would be only indirectly interested. . . . 'The Toilers,' must be read *by* the Toilers. It *must* be common; it must be vulgarized. (2:90–91)

Presley follows this advice, of course, and reaches a national audience, inspiring "revolutionary sermons, reactionary speeches," editorials, and advertisements "for patented cereals and infants' foods" (2:108). New York beckons, as it did to all the San Francisco artists of the nineties, but Presley "denied himself this cheap reward" (2:109). Yet he prepares for publication a book edition of *The Toilers and Other Poems*, collecting some of his earlier magazine work to fill out the volume. What could these earlier poems be, except toy-magazine pieces such as "The Better Part"?

In summary, Presley remains a paradoxical combination of strengths and weaknesses, an amalgam of cultural influences, and a would-be artist over whose characterization the novelist is always in control. His encounter with natural art involves four levels of experience: (1) a rejection of his previous poetic efforts of the *Lark* type, (2) a comparative analysis of juxtaposed aesthetic theories, made while living in the San Joaquin Valley; (3) a descent into contact with primordial nature and economic facts; and (4) an ascent enlivened by primeval experience but prevented from reaching Homeric heights by imperfect talent and vestiges of aestheticism.

After Presley, Vanamee is the most important artist in the novel. Yet he is an artist by decree rather than act; for, though a "poet by nature," he writes no poetry and therefore has no audience. His meaning as an artist is subordi-

92. "Salt and Sincerity," *The Complete Edition of Frank Norris*, 7:211.

nated to the problem of his personality. Like his fellow college graduates, Annixter and Presley, Vanamee undergoes a conversion from personal despair to universal optimism. As idea, Vanamee's conversion is acceptable. The function of the Vanamee-Angèle subplot is clear; in Charles L. Crow's words, "The return of Angèle, walking from the Seed Ranch across the fields of sprouting wheat, condenses the meaning of the novel, as Vanamee's last conversation with Presley reveals."[93] Moreover, much of Vanamee's characterization, as Crow has shown, derives from the influence of Bruce Porter and from various of his writings in the *Lark*. Specific Porter influences from the *Lark* include the persona of the mystical shepherd, the theme of the reproductive powers of nature and of man's smallness against nature's lofty benevolence, and the plot contrivance of good being brought forth out of death and evil.[94] Although Crow's arguments offer evidence that in this instance the *Lark* had a positive rather than a satirical influence upon *The Octopus*, there remain certain muted signs that impugn Vanamee's integrity and fail to square with Norris's thematic intentions.

Since Norris insists upon Vanamee's status as a "poet by nature," we are warranted in inquiring as to the meaning of Vanamee the artist. First of all, Vanamee looks like an artist, which in this novel means that he smacks of the studio. Indeed, in some respects he seems to be a disguised brother of Hartrath, with his "long black hair, such as one sees in the saints and evangelists of the pre-Raphaelite artists" (1:206). Even a passage that praises Vanamee's sensitivity comes very close to indicting him for the kind of unmanly aestheticism characteristic of Hartrath: "Living close to nature, a poet by instinct, where Presley was but a poet by training, there developed in him a great sensitiveness to beauty and an almost abnormal capacity for great happiness and great sorrow; he felt things intensely, deeply"

93. "The Real Vanamee and His Influence on Frank Norris' *The Octopus*," p. 131.
94. Ibid., pp. 135–39.

(1:33). His communion with nature is a plus, but the "great sensitiveness to beauty" and the "almost abnormal capacity" are rather like Hartrath's being unmanned by beauty. Further, Vanamee's contact with nature has not helped either his physical or mental health:

> The body was ill-nourished [from the desert sojourns], and the mind, concentrated forever upon one subject, had recoiled upon itself, had preyed upon the naturally nervous temperament, till the imagination had become exalted, morbidly active, diseased, beset with hallucinations, forever in search of the manifestation, of the miracle. (1:141)

In appearance, temperament, and vitality, Vanamee is not very different from effete city artists like Hartrath and Presley. The strongest claim for Vanamee as a natural artist therefore rests on certain of his aesthetic convictions: the need to reach a mass audience and the therefore necessary vulgarization of art; the confrontation with "primitive, simple, direct Life" (1:38); and the elevation of substance over form, with the greatest truth being "the primal heart of things" (2:90). All these ideas one finds throughout Norris's criticism.

Instead of existing as an artist, however, Vanamee lives the natural mode. He asks Presley, "But why write? Why not *live* in it? Steep oneself in the heat of the desert, the glory of the sunset, the blue haze of the mesa and the cañon" (1:39). Thus it is interesting that, once the central quest of his life is successfully concluded, once Angèle is restored to him, he should employ the language of literary genres to explain to Presley what has happened: "To put this story, this idyl, into words, would, for me, be a profanation" (2:345). But the story has of course been put into words— by Norris—and the words add up to something different in incident, style, and mood from everything else in the novel, as Norris himself fully understood, citing in a letter the "pure romance" of the "allegorical side of the wheat subject."[95] In two ways, however, the Vanamee idyl shares

95. Letter to Isaac F. Marcosson, 13 September 1900, *Letters*, p. 67.

with the stories of Annixter and Presley a common movement: the use of landscapes to effect the conversion from
false illusions to primal knowledge and the emphasis upon
"Reality" rather than "Romance." The stories of the three
young men are expressed in three generic modes: Gothic
romance (Vanamee), realism (Annixter), and pastoralism
(Presley). The latter two are successfully managed, but
Vanamee presents some problems.

As in a Gothic romance, Vanamee spends a great deal of
time, the better part of eighteen years, searching for his lost
sweetheart. The Mission, with its bats and moonlight and
exotic flowers and the mysterious Father Sarria,[96] excludes
the present reality of the world of railroads and ranchers,
sunlight and peasant maidens. One passage expresses this
generically typical isolation perfectly:

> It was a tiny corner of the great valley that stretched in all
> directions around it—shut off, discreet, romantic, a garden
> of dreams, of enchantments, of illusions. Outside there,
> far off, the great grim world went clashing through its grooves,
> but in here never an echo of the grinding of its wheels
> entered to jar upon the subdued modulation of the fountain's
> uninterrupted murmur. (1:135)

This garden is like Presley's early literary theory, which
would overlook the unpleasant facts of life. (And Angèle's
daughter, who should perhaps be called Angèle II, is, like
"The Toilers," derivative.) Angèle II cannot be summoned
from the garden; instead, she finally appears among the
realistic wheatfields. Her coming is a triumph of reality over
romance, the emergence of an actual girl to fulfill Vanamee's
desires:

> From out the world of romance, out of the moonlight
> and the star sheen, out of the faint radiance of the lilies
> and the still air heavy with perfume, she had at last come to
> him. The moonlight, the flowers, and the dream, were all
> vanished away. Angèle was realized in the Wheat. She stood
> forth in the sunlight, a fact, and no longer a fancy. (2:347)

96. Stuart L. Burns has identified Father Sarria as a Gothic villain
also, blaming him for the rape and subsequent death of Angèle. "The
Rapist in Frank Norris's *The Octopus*."

The deflation of Gothic romance into prosaic realism follows logically from Vanamee's aesthetic premises, and there is no mistaking his and Norris's preference: "The vision of the night had been beautiful, but what was it compared to this? Reality was better than Romance" (2:347). At the symbolic level, we have no trouble accepting the life-out-of-death import of the daughter's appearance. But at the literal level, we have a great deal, since the daughter who is supposed to be a "simple country girl" looks almost exactly like her mother, possessing the same "strange, balancing movement" of the head, the same eyes with an "oriental slant" and the same "enchanting fulness" of lips (2:347). As statement, she is a pastoral maiden; as image, she is still somewhat Gothic. What we feel, I think, is that Vanamee receives a kind of unearned validation of his conversion to optimism. He is rewarded with a specific, tangible prize, whereas Annixter gets killed (which in no way invalidates his convincingly realized love for Hilma and his newfound feeling of brotherhood for all men), and Presley goes on a lonely voyage to Asia. To cap everything, the daughter is not the mother, and there is something disturbing about Vanamee's willingness to accept the surrogate for the real thing. Analogically, the problem is that, although grains of wheat are interchangeable, human personalities are not.[97]

97. In defense of the Vanamee story line, James K. Folsom sees it as an ironic critique of a pseudo-good shepherd who misreads the parable from St. Paul and confuses the "natural" and the "spiritual." See "Social Darwinism or Social Protest? The 'Philosophy' of *The Octopus*." There is nothing in the language of the subplot to suggest irony, however, nor is irony of situation present as in the scenes juxtaposing Mrs. Hooven's death by starvation with the Gerard banquet. For a much more convincing defense of the significance and utility of the Vanamee story, see Richard Allan Davison, "Frank Norris' *The Octopus*: Some Observations on Vanamee, Shelgrim and St. Paul," pp. 190–95. Admitting some difficulties in the Vanamee plot, Davison makes the best case yet for the spiritual qualities symbolized by the shepherd and shows that he is intended to serve as a moral "barometer" (p. 193). For an extensive discussion of multiple genres in *The Octopus*, see William L. Vance, "Romance in *The Octopus*." Vance judges the novel a failure because of the presence of what he regards as incompatible literary modes.

The third young man in the novel, Annixter, is the least aesthetic minded but the one who experiences the most satisfactory aesthetic emotion. Conceived at a comically realistic level—the sign of which is that he is always reading *David Copperfield*—Annixter is a college-trained anti-intellectual with a grudging, humorous respect for the mysteries of art:

> No doubt, there was not much use in poetry, and as for novels, to his mind, there were only Dickens's works. Everything else was a lot of lies. But just the same, it took brains to grind out a poem. It wasn't everyone who could rhyme "brave" and "glaive," and make sense out of it. (1:24)

His room, described in detail, has very few aesthetic objects, only some lithographs and some withered flowers; it is "essentially a man's room, rugged, uncouth, virile" (1:155). By comparison, Presley's room is a tasteful, conscious version of Annixter's untutored simplicity. Its appointments are "of the simplest," and only two pictures adorn the walls, "one a reproduction of the Reading from Homer, the other a charcoal drawing of the Mission of San Juan de Guadalajara, which Presley had made himself" (2:84). These details express Presley's constant admiration for Homer (whom he is never able to approach in artistry) and his interest in Spanish California (out of which he is capable of creating art of a conventional kind). Presley's room fulfills late fin-de-siècle preferences for simplicity and anti-bric-à-brac decor: "It amused and interested him to maintain its air of rigorous simplicity and freshness. He abhorred cluttered bric-à-brac and meaningless *objets d' art*" (2:84–85).

The difference between Presley's tastes and Annixter's is comically dramatized in a description of the furnishings of Annixter's and Hilma's married home. After their wedding in San Francisco, Hilma purchases the appointments for their new household. She apparently shops at the same department store as Trina and the Wade family, since when Presley visits them he sees decor that makes him hasten "to change the subject":

> Presley looked at the marvellous, department-store bed of brass, with its brave, gay canopy; the mill-made washstand, with its pitcher and bowl of blinding red and green china, the straw-framed lithographs of symbolic female figures against the multi-coloured new wall-paper, the inadequate spindle chairs of white and gold; the sphere of tissue paper hanging from the gas fixture, and the plumes of pampas grass tacked to the wall at artistic angles, and overhanging two astonishing oil paintings, in dazzling golden frames. (2:179)

Obviously we are in the presence once again of the "Home Book of Art" style and of the cheaply manufactured art so heavily criticized in *Vandover* and *McTeague*. Yet their bad taste has nothing to do with ethical stature; for Hilma and Annixter, together and separately, are the heroes of the novel. Hilma, through her pastoral-maiden qualities of innocence and simple (while intensely physical) beauty, converts Annixter from selfishness and seduction to love, marriage, and brotherhood. His revelatory moment, in the wheatfields at dawn, is a triumph of emotion over will, and it comes to him with the power of an intense aesthetic experience: "Instantly, like the swift blending of beautiful colours, like the harmony of beautiful chords of music, the two ideas melted into one, and in that moment into his harsh, unlovely world a new idea was born" (2:81). Hilma is in a sense the novel's answer to the phony milkmaid of Hartrath's painting. We see her standing in the dairy wreathed in a corona of sunlight; we see her gathering watercress beside a cool stream.

More than any of Norris's other novels, *The Octopus* is a novel of landscapes; hence it is essentially pastoral in its movements and harmonies. The pattern is apparent from the beginning. Presley, the city artist, has come to the country to try to develop a more vigorous and Homeric art. To do so he must understand the nature of man's relationship with the landscape. His problem is stated baldly in the first chapter:

> On one hand, it was his ambition to portray life as he saw it—directly, frankly, and through no medium of personality

or temperament. But, on the other hand, as well, he wished to
see everything through a rose-coloured mist—a mist that
dulled all harsh outlines, all crude and violent colours. . . .
He had set himself the task of giving true, absolutely true,
poetical expression to the life of the ranch, and yet, again
and again, he brought up against the railroad, that stubborn
iron barrier against which his romance shattered itself to
froth and disintegrated, flying spume. (1:10)

This passage encapsulates Norris's own growth as an
artist, expressing the need to achieve a dialectical resolution
to the conflicting claims of romance and realism and raising
the problem of finding technical strategies for conveying
both objective and subjective aspects of a situation. But Norris is describing a condition that he surely must have believed
himself to have already solved.

Presley's dilemma is developed in pathetic terms at the
end of chapter 1: the sheep are slaughtered by the train,
thus bringing into reality the "terrible, formless" shapes that
troubled his musings (1:44). Much later, in preparation for
the climax of the novel's action, Norris returns Presley to
this very hillside, where, in the company of his rancher
friends, he hears the news that the armed railroad men are
coming to dispossess the ranchers. Now the harmony of the
landscape is disrupted in tragic terms, as men from both
sides, eight in all, die in a fierce gunfight. Such are the violent
disruptions of men's potentially peaceful and fruitful relationships with landscapes and with each other, of the kind
of pastoral stasis that Hilma and Annixter attain. There are
also moments that lyrically celebrate the people living close
to the land. In such a passage as the following, pastoral
stasis is merged with Homeric primitivism to show Presley
in rapt aesthetic control of perceptions that would once have
repulsed him. The occasion is a feast held after a bloody
communal rabbit hunt:

> Presley was delighted with it all. It was Homeric, this feast-
> ing, this vast consuming of meat and bread and wine, followed
> now by games of strength. An epic simplicity and directness,
> an honest Anglo-Saxon mirth and innocence, commended it.
> Crude it was; coarse it was, but no taint of viciousness was

here. These people were good people, kindly, benignant even, always readier to give than to receive, always more willing to help than to be helped. They were good stock. Of such was the backbone of the nation—sturdy Americans every one of them. Where else in the world round were such strong, honest men, such strong, beautiful women? (2:216–17)

Presley's insights into coarse experience and his acceptance of man's primal needs represent considerable growth on his part. He has come some distance from his earlier queasiness before the unpleasant facts of ranch life. After appreciating the strength and vitality of the men and women of the wheat country, Presley again returns to the city, where he encounters their opposites, aesthetes and bloodless daughters of the rich amidst a setting far removed from the San Joaquin Valley. The scene, which takes place at the Gerard mansion on Nob Hill, brings to a climax the evaluation of landscapes.

In the company of Mrs. Cedarquist, Presley attends a sumptuous dinner given by the wealthy Mrs. Gerard, a society woman and patroness of the arts. Norris apparently got the idea for the scene from a newspaper account of a banquet held at the mansion of John Miller, a man in the employ of Collis P. Huntington's Central Pacific Railroad. Miller was able to possess many fine things, Huntington discovered, because he had been embezzling funds from the company. Disclosure led to Miller's suicide. But only the banquet found its way into *The Octopus*. The newspaper story, pasted in Norris's *Octopus* notebook, reads thus:

> The banquet was a notable one. All the great railroad magnates were there. The wines were of the rarest vintages. The service was irreproachable, the viands fit for a Roman orgie—in the days of the decadence. The magnates clinked glasses with John Miller. They responded to toasts with flattering allusions to his ability and faithful service. They complimented him on his home, its furnishings, his pictures, statuary, servants, his dinner.[98]

Robert Lundy, who is very critical of Norris's use of this source, thinks that he "fell victim to the breathless tone

---

98. "Notes. I." Quoted by permission of Director, Bancroft Library.

and stereotypical conception of the journalist."[99] It is hard
to see how this is the case, however. The brief newspaper
description becomes in Norris's handling a scene stretching
over several pages and loaded with specific description and
concreteness absent from the reporter's summary account.
Indeed, so much has been transformed that the newspaper
story is merely a starting point; and Norris, far from being
a captive of its rhetoric, has converted the sketch into a characteristic example of his aesthetic documentation.

To this source Norris added his personal knowledge of
a house singularly appropriate for this scene. As Donald
Pizer has observed, the Gerard mansion seems to be based
upon one of the mansions of the Big Four, all of whom had
houses on Nob Hill.[100] The Mark Hopkins mansion is the
most likely candidate.[101] Converted into an art museum in
1893, the Mark Hopkins Institute was one of the best-known
landmarks of San Francisco in the nineties. It was, according
to architectural historian Harold Kirker, the "last and worst
of the railroad palaces."[102] Les Jeunes would have agreed
with this estimate. Bruce Porter condemned its interior
architecture, calling it "one of those monstrous creations of
the architect, the decorator and the upholsterer."[103] Burgess
counted it one of the "architectural monstrosities" of the
city.[104] Norris was also critical of the Hopkins house, writing
in 1897 that it was "miserably adapted to the uses of a gallery."[105] In the novel, however, the exterior is not described,
and the interior is presented in attractive terms. Norris describes two of its rooms with the kind of elaborate documentation that constitutes, as we have seen in *Vandover* and
McTeague, one of his favorite fictional strategies:

99. "The Making of *McTeague* and *The Octopus*," p. 256.
100. *The Novels of Frank Norris*, p. 122.
101. Ibid.
102. *California's Architectural Frontier: Style and Tradition in the Nineteenth Century*, p. 94.
103. "The Winter Exhibition: The Hopkins House a Failure as an Art Gallery."
104. "Architectural Shams: The Efforts of San Francisco Architects to Achieve the Impossible."
105. "Pictures To Burn."

The room was very large, and of excessive loftiness. Flat, rectagonal pillars of a rose-tinted, variegated marble rose from the floor almost flush with the walls, finishing off at the top with gilded capitals of a Corinthian design, which supported the ceiling. The ceiling itself, instead of joining the walls at right angles, curved to meet them, a device that produced a sort of dome-like effect. This ceiling was a maze of golden involutions in very high relief, that adjusted themselves to form a massive framing for a great picture, nymphs and goddesses, white doves, golden chariots, and the like, all wreathed about with clouds and garlands of roses. Between the pillars around the sides of the room were hangings of silk, the design—of a Louis Quinze type—of beautiful simplicity and faultless taste. The fireplace was a marvel. It reached from floor to ceiling; the lower parts, black marble, carved into crouching Atlases, with great muscles that upbore the superstructure. The design of this latter, of a kind of purple marble, shot through with white veinings, was in the same style as the design of the silk hangings. In its midst was a bronze escutcheon, bearing an undecipherable monogram and a Latin motto. Andirons of brass, nearly six feet high, flanked the hearthstone.

The windows of the room were heavily draped in sombre brocade and *écru* lace, in which the initials of the family were very beautifully worked. But directly opposite the fireplace, an extra window, lighted from the adjoining conservatory, threw a wonderful, rich light into the apartment. It was a Gothic window of stained glass very large, the centre figures being armed warriors, Parsifal and Lohengrin; the one with a banner, the other with a swan. The effect was exquisite, the window a veritable masterpiece, glowing, flaming, and burning with a hundred tints and colours—opalescent, purple, wine-red, clouded pinks, royal blues, saffrons, violets so dark as to be almost black.

Under foot, the carpet had all the softness of texture of grass; skins (one of them of an enormous polar bear) and rugs of silk velvet were spread upon the floor. A Renaissance cabinet of ebony, many feet taller than Presley's head, and inlaid with ivory and silver, occupied one corner of the room, while in its centre stood a vast table of Flemish oak, black, heavy as iron, massive. A faint odour of sandalwood pervaded the air. From the conservatory near by came the splashing of a fountain. A row of electric bulbs let into the frieze of the walls, between the golden capitals, and burning dimly behind hemispheres of clouded glass, threw a subdued light over the whole scene. (2:300–301)

The dining room is described less copiously but not less concretely:

> The dining room was superb in its appointments. On three sides of the room, to the height of some ten feet, ran a continuous picture, an oil painting, divided into long sections by narrow panels of black oak. The paintings represented the personages in the *Roman de la Rose,* and was conceived in an atmosphere of the most delicate, most ephemeral allegory. One saw young chevaliers, blue-eyed, of elemental beauty and purity; women with crowns, gold girdles, and cloudy wimples; young girls, entrancing in their loveliness, wearing snow-white kerchiefs, their golden hair unbound and flowing, dressed in white samite, bearing armfuls of flowers; the whole procession defiling against a background of forest glades, venerable oaks, half-hidden fountains, and fields of asphodel and roses.
>
> Otherwise, the room was simple. Against the side of the wall unoccupied by the picture stood a sideboard of gigantic size that once had adorned the banquet hall of an Italian palace of the late Renaissance. It was black with age, and against its sombre surfaces glittered an array of heavy silver dishes and heavier cut-glass bowls and goblets. (2:311)

The extent to which Norris supplied new details for the interior and drew upon the basic features of the Hopkins Institute can be seen in contemporary descriptions of the Hopkins decor. The hall, which appears to be the first room in the descriptions quoted above, was described thus in an official catalog:

> The walls are finished to the ceiling almost entirely in oak, inlaid with ebony, yamana and other woods, elaborately carved in detail. . . . Springing from this frieze is a cove-ceiling which curves to the skylight above, on the east and west sides of which G. Baribaldi has painted, against a background of deep blue diapered with gold, symbolical figures of the fine arts; and on the north and south side the great masters. . . . The eight panels in this screen are filled with decorations by California and Italian artists, illustrating

different phases of architectural design from the Assyrian to modern times.[106]

The elaborate decorative effects of the original have been heightened and altered in Norris's treatment. He has changed the content of the mural and added details about silk hangings, the fireplace, and the like. The catalog description of the dining room shows a similar relationship between the Hopkins Institute and the Gerard house:

> The room is also floored with hardwood laid in geometric design and is entirely furnished in English elac; the buffets, mantel piece, deep wainscoting, ceiling beams and panels being entirely of this material very richly carved and decorated. Between wainscoting and ceiling is a decorated frieze in gold and color by E. Naijot, representing the harvest, vintage, hunting, fishing, etc.[107]

As a self-contained unit considered for its own merits, the interior that Norris describes *is* beautiful. The silk hangings are of "a beautiful simplicity and faultless taste"; the family initials in the ecru lace are "very beautifully worked"; the stained-glass window is a "veritable masterpiece"; the dining room is "superb." On this last point a contemporary observer, A. Altschvl, agreed; he declared the dining room to be "very beautiful, and a perfectly consistent and harmonious piece of interior decoration."[108] Even a possibly pejorative phrase of Norris's like "excessive loftiness" is rendered merely descriptive as the various effects of the house—the lofty ceiling, the cabinet taller than Presley—support what Altschvl called the "general impression of grandeur, of largeness and splendor."[109] Proportionally, the Gerard interior possesses intrinsic aesthetic harmony. As a whole it violates none of Norris's aesthetic canons, including simplicity.

The thematic implications of the decor are rich indeed. This is a home of gods, of creatures beyond the touch of

106. San Francisco Art Association, *Spring Exhibition.*
107. Ibid.
108. "The Mark Hopkins Institute Of Art."
109. Ibid.

daily care or the press of hunger. Everything is gigantic; the effect is of enormous size, but of size under control. All of nature—the polar bear, light, even fire—is subject to technological and aesthetic manipulation. This is a palace of art, containing eclectic pleasures and insulated from the hurly-burly world beyond its walls. The Gerard house is a palace of art in another respect too. The allegorical scenes in the murals represent idealized chevaliers and lovely maidens in an idyllically pastoral landscape. The effect is a kind of higher sentimentality. Since none of the scenes described can be found in *The Romance of the Rose*, Norris's use of this title seems to be misleading. It is possible that he was in error, of course, or that he had a painting in mind rather than the medieval poem. Whatever the explanation, the relevance of the title is obvious. *The Romance of the Rose* echoes Presley's search among California antiquity for the materials of art. Its use here also corresponds very closely with Norris's critical position regarding a major fallacy that weakened historical romances of the period. In 1902 he attacked the tendency to relegate romance to distant times, especially to the Middle Ages and the Renaissance:

> Lately you have been taking Romance a weary journey across the water—ages and the flood of years—and hailing her into the fusby, musty, worm-eaten, moth-riddled, rust-corroded Grandes Salles of the Middle Ages and the Renaissance, and she has found the drama of a bygone age for you there.[110]

Art in the Gerard mansion is similarly isolated from the reality of contemporary life. This insulation, symbolized by the cold pastoralism of the murals, is underlined by action and dialogue. Thus, the unreal allegory of the murals is deliberately contrasted, in the rhetoric of allegory, with a "real" allegory being enacted in the streets outside the Gerard mansion. Mrs. Hooven and her infant are moving toward their appointed death by starvation in front of the Gerard dwelling: "Death is at the end of that devious, winding maze of paths, crossed and recrossed and crossed again.

110. "A Plea For Romantic Fiction."

There is but one goal to the *via dolorosa*" (2:304). Perhaps the most telling single detail is Mrs. Gerard's discourse on the freshness of the asparagus, delivered that day by special train from the San Joaquin Valley.[111] We recall the Derricks' troubles in getting plows delivered to their ranch and Hilma gathering watercress in a marshy stream beneath a railroad trestle. The violation of the pastoral landscape could hardly be more effectively presented.

The principal observer at the dinner scene is of course Presley, and what he sees both irresistibly appeals to his aesthetic impulses and disturbs his newly acquired social and moral beliefs. At the dinner table, over talk of Xeres 1815 wine (the Gerards scorn California wines), Presley is moved to a "fancy, . . . distorted, caricatured, terrible":

> Harran, Annixter, and Hooven were being devoured there under his eyes. These dainty women, his cousin Beatrice and little Miss Gerard, frail, delicate; all these fine ladies with their small fingers and slender necks, suddenly were trans-figured in his tortured mind into harpies tearing human flesh. (2:317)

Although Presley is thinking in characteristically melodramatic images, there is something sound in his basic perception; the natural relationship of these people to the landscape and its fruits is distorted and grotesque. The daughters, for example, are unhealthy counterparts to earth mothers like Hilma Tree. They and the "languid" Julian Lambert, another version of the aesthete, are the very symbols of the degeneration so feared in the nineties, the decade in which Max Nordau's *Degeneration* was a best-seller (2:311). The same types that Norris attacks in *The Octopus* and everywhere in his criticism are also criticized, for example, by a *Wave* diatribe:

> The desire of the jeunesse doré to adopt pretty little ways, to flourish well manicured hands, to wear elaborate underwear, dainty slippers, silk-lined smoking jackets, expensive

111. Lundy, in "The Making of *McTeague* and *The Octopus*," finds the dialogue about the asparagus a "parody of speech" and believes the entire dinner scene "incredible on the realistic level" (p. 257).

pantaloons of soft velvet, is as much signs of degeneration as the curled and perfumed moustaches, the scented cigarettes, the pale bejewelled hands from which the blood is shaken, and the pink ears.[112]

After experiencing the vision of cannibalism, which is a violent image of the complicity that is, after all, a central social theme in the novel, Presley behaves in his usual fashion in the presence of wealth and power and beauty; he is polite, he says nothing. The Gerard dinner, often condemned for its melodrama or praised for its irony, is thus of even more importance as a final symbolic commentary on the social and aesthetic education of the central figure in the novel, Presley.

Presley's philosophical education, however, is another matter. Despite his artistic inadequacies, Presley is granted the major role of reflecting the last viewpoint presented in the novel. Similarly, Vanamee, described throughout as a mystic and a Hebrew-like prophet, is given crucial speeches affirming the optimistic interpretation of human suffering. The reason for this disjunction between artistic mediocrity or inconsistency and philosophical accuracy and authenticity —from Norris's point of view, of course—would seem to lie in considerations outside the novel proper. Norris's personal war against cultist art, salons, dilettantism, against anything that smacked of effete aestheticism, was at its most intense at the turn of the century. He liked to present himself as a bourgeois professional novelist; and in the newspaper articles written in 1901–1902, both those collected in *The Responsibilities of the Novelist* (1903) and others, he relentlessly attacked litterateurs and poseurs. Only in his last novel, *The Pit* (1903), was he able to present an artist without also presenting the deep suspicions discoverable in the portraits of Presley and Vanamee.

To return to the ending of *The Octopus* is to confront the major critical debate about this novel.[113] It is not my purpose

112. "Splashes," *Wave* 14 (20 April 1895): 11.

113. For a compact survey of the major reviews and articles, see Richard Allan Davison, ed., *The Merrill Studies in The Octopus.*

here to review the arguments and counterarguments about the integrity of the closing rhetoric—that "all things, surely, inevitably, resistlessly work together for good" (2:361)—rather I intend to describe a structural element that ties together the patterns of despair converted to optimism that occur in the lives of Annixter, Vanamee, and Presley. In each case a woman is integral to the young man's growth. With respect to Annixter and Vanamee, this statement is hardly news. For the last twenty years Norris criticism, especially the work of Donald Pizer and William B. Dillingham, has disclosed key elements of structural unity in the parallel conversions of Annixter and Vanamee, the first from personal selfishness to love for Hilma Tree, the second from personal despair to cosmic optimism that springs from the rediscovery of the lost Angèle in the person of her daughter.[114] In each instance, the particular rebirth of love and hope is accompanied by a more general metaphysical dimension, felt by Annixter and articulated in didactic language by Vanamee, as befits his status as seer and crypto-artist.

What has not been recognized is Presley's similar contact with a woman. In the much-debated closing scenes critical emphasis always focuses on one or more of three events: Presley's interview with Shelgrim; the last meeting with Vanamee, who delivers his message of optimism to Presley; and the meditation at the end, as Presley stands alone on the deck of the *Swanhilda*, recalling the words of Vanamee and his cosmic faith in the irresistible working out of good and the sure accomplishment of the perfect whole. But preceding the last two of these scenes is Presley's final visit to the wheat country. The harvest season is over; various defeated

---

For Davison's own opinion about the conclusion of the novel, see his "Frank Norris' *The Octopus*: Some Observations on Vanamee, Shelgrim and St. Paul."

114. Pizer concentrates on the relationship between the cycle of growing wheat and the human perception of love and rebirth (*The Novels of Frank Norris*, pp. 131–33); Dillingham, on the relationship between man's instinct and his instinctual growth in nature through the ascendancy of feeling over intellect (*Frank Norris: Instinct and Art*, pp. 63–65).

survivors of the tragic struggle—Magnus Derrick and his wife, for example—are dispiritedly trying to carry on; and rampant over all is the "Master of the Wheat," S. Behrman (2:324). The most affecting creature of all is Annixter's widow, Hilma Tree. Presley talks with her and experiences an emotion remarkably kindred to the one that had moved Annixter to realize his love for her. Presley, too, undergoes a genuine conversion of the heart, sparked by emotion and corroborated by intellect:

> A longing to give the best that was in him to the memory of her, to be strong and noble because of her, to reshape his purposeless, half-wasted life with her nobility and purity and gentleness for his inspiration leaped all at once within him, leaped and stood firm, hardening to a resolve stronger than any he had ever known. (2:338)

Immediately afterward, Presley realizes that this is not one of his characteristically impulsive responses, that on the contrary he has been strongly drawn to Hilma from the first time he met her. Then, responding to her melancholy bearing, he delivers his most sensitive and helpful speech in the novel. Paralyzed by her grief for Annixter, Hilma cannot be happy. But Presley's message contains wisdom, perspective, and pragmatism; he tells her to remember Annixter but to commit herself to life and the future: "Your sorrow need not be a burden to you. If you consider it as you should— as you *will* some day, believe me—it will only be a great help to you. It will make you more noble, a truer woman, more generous" (2:339). This view, which honors present temporal suffering but insists upon a longer, more hopeful view of the impermanence of human suffering, may bother contemporary critics because of its generalized optimism, but it should not bother their sense of formal consistency. For Presley's musings at the end are merely orotund and Vanamee-influenced expansions of the basic optimism that he here shares with Hilma Annixter. The pattern, from emotionally felt and personally experienced stirrings of the heart to intellectual formulations, matches perfectly the Vanamee model. Presley's cosmic optimism is thus an earned and prepared-for conclusion. And to punctuate sensationally the upward swing at the end, we recall that S. Behrman, master of the wheat, is buried beneath tons of wheat in the ship's hold.[115]

Whether Presley can experience a similar growth in artistic powers is not clear. Donald Pizer, virtually the only critic to note the scene between Presley and Hilma, detects a hint that "with the aid of a strong woman he [Presley] might . . . reinforce his temperament and prove himself as an artist."[116] But as I have argued above, Presley the human being qua philosopher is kept quite distinct from Presley the artist, who remains tainted with the lavender tarbrush of elite aestheticism.

Most discussions of *The Octopus*, no matter how critical or faultfinding they are, end with paeans to Norris's vast canvas, his breadth of intentions, his almost-great accomplishment. It is my contention that examination of the aesthetic background yields a renewed respect for Norris's accomplishment, both in discrete details and general conception. *The Octopus* is truly one of the most considerable efforts by an American writer to embrace what Norris spoke of in an essay as "the huge conglomerate West."[117]

---

115. In a recent essay James K. Folsom has interpreted S. Behrman as a principle of animal energy (bear-man). Thus, his presence on Presley's ship represents a part of life that Presley, who acknowledges only the vegetable (the wheat), fails to recognize. "The Wheat and the Locomotive: Norris and Naturalistic Esthetics," p. 72.

116. *The Novels of Frank Norris*, p. 136.

117. " 'The Literature of the West': A Reply to W. R. Lighton." The best discussion to date of Norris's effort to capture a West that is both urban and rural is Glen A. Love's "Frank Norris's Western Metropolitans." Love offers a useful corrective to the view of Norris as a conventional pastoral writer espousing the country over the city; he argues instead that "Norris's western metropolis is . . . the emblem of an inevitable future, urban and complex, in which the survivors are those who have met the city's strenuous and unique requirements" (p. 4).

The Drama of *The Pit*

Vandover and the Brute, McTeague, and *The Octopus*
each involved Norris in a topography he knew well: San
Francisco and the valleys and deserts south of the city. Moreover, each drew upon specific aesthetic issues and facts that
arose from Norris's intimate contact with the local artistic
scene. But *The Pit* (1903), with its Chicago setting, represented something of a new departure. Still, Chicago could
scarcely be considered an unknown city to Norris, who after
all had spent the first fourteen years of his life there and
quite possibly had returned there briefly in 1893 to attend
the Chicago World's Fair.[1] Therefore, in 1901 when he and
his wife visited the city for background research on *The
Pit,* he was hardly entering foreign territory. Besides, Chicago was not so different from San Francisco in three respects:
it too, even more than San Francisco, was a monument to
American commercial energy; it was indubitably a Western
city; and it possessed a lively aesthetic milieu. It also offered a personal dimension for Norris, if we are to credit the
two central character portrayals in the novel. According to
Charles G. Norris, Curtis Jadwin and Laura Dearborn were
clearly modeled upon Norris's father and mother.[2] From details such as Jadwin's admiration for the nationally popular
preacher Dwight Moody, to the art treasures contained in
their dwelling, Jadwin and Laura sprang from Norris's
personal experience.

Yet *The Pit* is also quite different from its predecessors
in several ways. Although the density of its aesthetic documentation is as great as that of *Vandover,* which statistically

1. This assumption is based upon specific allusions to the fair in
Norris's journalism; see, for example, "Re-Creating a University:
The Great Project of Reconstructing the College of Berkeley" and
"In the Compound of a Diamond Mine." Of course he could have got
his impressions from photographs and printed accounts also.

2. Letter to Franklin Walker, 1 November 1930. Franklin Walker
Collection, Bancroft Library, Berkeley, Calif. Cited by permission of
Director, Bancroft Library.

contains more references than either *McTeague* or *The Octopus*, the references are of a different kind. In *Vandover*, painting and architecture, both exterior and interior, predominate; in *McTeague*, popular culture, interior decor, and landscapes; in *The Octopus*, local artists, actual literary issues, and landscapes. In *The Pit*, however, music, literature of a national dimension, and drama comprise the major sources of aesthetic documentation. Two of these sources, it is true, have their roots in Norris's early experience. He attended operas in Paris and later in San Francisco, which offered a lively opera scene in the 1890s.[3] There is even stronger evidence of a keen interest in drama. Norris attended plays in San Francisco and New York; reviewed a few for the *Wave*; interviewed prominent actors and actresses and playwrights such as Augustus Thomas, James A. Herne, and David Belasco; and even acted in a play himself on at least one occasion: a charity performance of *Caste* in 1897.[4]

Aesthetic material is also handled a bit differently in *The Pit*. Literary allusions, for example, are more profuse and reflect Norris's public preoccupation with the novel, as opposed to his earlier interest in architecture and painting. Such allusions are also less disguised or less covert than in *The Octopus* and are consequently less personal. Further, the rhetoric of aesthetic documentation in this novel is somehow more transparent than in the earlier works such as *Vandover*; in other words, there is less a sense of an underground network of imagery. Instead, allusions in *The Pit* function as a direct guide and commentary.

Possible explanations for this "new" Norris novel may be offered. For one thing, in *The Pit* he sought to explore a

3. One opera it is certain he saw in San Francisco was *L'Africaine*, since he wrote a *Wave* piece about the troupe: "The French Opera: Characteristics of the Troupe as Revealed in 'L'Africaine.'" His article about student days in Paris, "Student Life in Paris," mentions several composers, including Gounod and Verdi.

4. For an account of this episode, see D. B. Graham, "Frank Norris, Actor."

class of people heretofore untreated in his fiction. Interestingly, this class is similar to the one that vitiates the hero's talent in the important short story "Dying Fires": "The leisure class, opera-goers, intriguers."[5] *The Pit* also enters directly into Howells country, and some readers have suggested certain affinities with *The Rise of Silas Lapham,* including a businessman hero whose duplicity leads him into financial ruin but moral growth,[6] a subplot involving young lovers, and the symbolic use of houses to measure states of spiritual malfeasance.[7] A third explanation is that *The Pit* represents Norris's long-standing critical view that the construction of a novel has its direct analogue in the construction of drama.[8] It is this last point that *The Pit* most exemplifies, for in this work the aesthetic documentation creates a truly dramatic or dramalike novel.

In an essay in 1901 Norris claimed that the construction of a novel should be predicated on the classic, Aristotelian model:

> The axiom, "The whole is greater than the part," is as true for a novel as it is for a proposition of geometry. He [the writer] could be shown that the divisions of the drama—i. e., (1) the start, (2) the rise, (3) the height, (4) the close—are equally essential to the novel and conducive to the readers' interest—which is always the same as artistic finish.[9]

His familiarity with such principles of construction probably had more humble origins than Aristotle, however. For example, in an interview with David Belasco in 1897, Norris

---

5. Frank Norris, *The Complete Edition of Frank Norris,* 4:123.

6. Janie Helen Blitch, "*The Pit* and Allusive Revelations," p. 39.

7. Charles G. Hoffman briefly suggests comparing these two novels in "Norris and the Responsibility of the Novelist," p. 513.

8. In an important essay on the art of *The Octopus* Richard Allan Davison has also pointed to the kinship between Norris's idea of unity and "the structural patterns of . . . Greek tragedy." ("Frank Norris' *The Octopus*: Some Observations on Vanamee, Shelgrim and St. Paul," p. 187).

9. "Frank Norris' Weekly Letter," *Chicago American Art and Literary Review,* 8 June 1901, p. 5.

heard the famous playwright explain the importance of the "careful preparation that makes all the difference between melodrama and drama."[10] Belasco's elaboration is extremely pertinent to the points Norris made in his essay: "Preparation for your effects; gradual, natural, leading up to them, coaxing your audience step by step till you have them just where you want, and then spring your effect, and not until then."[11] In another article Norris reduces the first part of Belasco's statement to the phrase "preparation of effect."[12] Also relevant is Norris's thorough dissection of Winston Churchill's novel *The Crisis* (1901), which he judges a failure because of its lack of proper dramatic construction and its consequent diffusion of potential dramatic power: "It seems to me that this diffuseness, the scattering and partitioning of the drama, is the weakest point in Mr. Churchill's novel. Where is the grouping? Just what is the writer trying to show? Upon what peg does he hang his story? Up to what pivotal scene does he lead?"[13]

There is some interesting external and intentional evidence of Norris's preoccupation with drama during the writing of *The Pit*. For one thing, drama was on Norris's mind in 1901–1902 because the daughter and widow of playwright James A. Herne wanted to collaborate with him on a dramatization of *The Octopus*.[14] More importantly, Norris left a record of his intentions in writing *The Pit* in the form of a letter that explicitly sets forth the dramatic nature of the novel. Perhaps anticipating possible criticism of the novel for its lack of focus on the wheat and the Jadwin

10. "Belasco on Plays: The Great Playwright Speaks of his Methods."

11. Ibid. One of Belasco's plays mentioned in this interview is *The Wife*, which presents a plot situation somewhat like that of *The Pit*: a husband asks an unfaithful wife to turn to him for comfort and continued affection.

12. "The Mechanics of Fiction."

13. "Frank Norris' Weekly Letter," *Chicago American Art and Literary Review*, 22 June 1901, p. 8.

14. *The Letters of Frank Norris*, ed. Franklin Walker, p. 80.

material, a charge still leveled against it,[15] he explained his intentions:

> The story is told through Laura Dearborn. *She occupies the center of the stage all the time,* and I shall try to interest the reader more in the problems of her character and career than in any other human element in the book. The two main themes, consequently, are the story of Jadwin's corner of May wheat and the story of his wife's "affair" with Corthell.
>
> I shall try to show that all these are American issues, modern, typical and important. The "big scenes" will be the scene between Laura and Corthell in her apartments the evening that Jadwin fails to appear, and the scene on the floor of the Chicago Board of Trade when the Jadwin corner breaks.[16]

By insisting on the novel's dramatic qualities and the necessity of seeing Laura, not Jadwin, as the central figure, Norris was clearly indicating that his concept of this novel was quite different from the expectations held by readers looking for another *Octopus*. The center of interest in Norris's realistic drama, then, is Laura Jadwin; and her story is the familiar one in Norris of perceptual confusion. Through aesthetic reference—especially dramatic analogy—Laura's dilemma is revealed: she does not know who she is and she cannot reconcile aesthetic experience with other kinds of experience.

15. For example, Charles C. Walcutt says, "In *The Pit* there are two stories, and the naturalistic setting applies to only one of them" (*American Literary Naturalism: A Divided Stream*, p. 155). James D. Hart agrees that "the themes of *The Pit* are several and their fusion is not always well achieved" (Introduction to *The Pit*, p. viii). Two critics who rate *The Pit* as the best of Norris's work are Larzer Ziff and Warren French. Ziff argues that *The Pit* contains a "psychological penetration missing from *The Octopus*" (*The American 1890s: Life and Times of A Lost Generation*, p. 271). French believes that "the novel is more carefully thought out than its predecessor and is, in fact, the only work in which Norris shows promise of achieving intellectual maturity" (*Frank Norris*, p. 107).

16. Letter to Isaac Marcosson, November 1901, in "Ten Letters By Frank Norris," ed. Donald Pizer, pp. 59–60.

9

interesting
Combination

Thus Norris's last novel most resembles his first, with *Vandover* and *The Pit* forming one body of inquiry, and the middle novels, *McTeague* and *The Octopus*, another. In *Vandover* and *The Pit* Norris presents characters divided between a confident belief in art and an ambiguous involvement in aesthetic experience. The ambiguities confronting such characters, the affirmative and dangerous possibilities of aesthetic experience, are his true subject. In *McTeague* and *The Octopus* aesthetic experience in the form of conventional art is again under attack, but in both the emphasis falls upon an alternative aesthetic source, nature and Western landscapes. It is interesting to note that the novel that is most confident about the value of aesthetic experience is the one Norris was least involved in personally, *McTeague*. *The Pit*, which returns Norris to the personal fires of *Vandover*, represents a triumph of control over the privately challenging questions of art and aesthetic experience.

In the opening chapter, which introduces the principal motifs of aesthetic experience, Norris presents Laura as a theatrical heroine:

> And all this beauty of pallid face and brown eyes was crowned by, and sharply contrasted with, the intense blackness of her hair, abundant, thick, extremely heavy, continually coruscating with sombre, murky reflections, tragic, in a sense vaguely portentous—the coiffure of a heroine of romance, doomed to dark crises.[17]

She is both dramatic (tragic) and melodramatic, for the label "heroine of romance" echoes novels of the day, romances such as Ouida's *Wanda*, which is one of Laura's favorite novels. The heroine of *Wanda* is to a considerable degree an idealization of what Laura would like to be and to a dangerous extent is. It is easy to see why she would have admired Ouida's heroine:

> The Countess Wanda van Szahar was a beautiful woman; but she had that supreme distinction which eclipses beauty, that subtle, indescribable grace and dignity which are never

17. *The Complete Edition of Frank Norris*, 9:2. Hereafter, all citations from *The Pit* are to this edition and will be included in the text.

seen apart from some great lineage with long traditions of culture, courtesy, and courage. She was very tall, and her movements had a great repose and harmony in them; her figure, richness and symmetry. . . . She was one of the most beautiful women of her country, and one of the most courted and the most flattered. Perhaps she is rather too far from human emotions and human needs. The women of the house of Szahar have been mostly very proud, silent, brave, and resolute; great ladies rather than lovable wives.[18]

Laura is like the countess in beauty, aristocratic bearing, and self-pride. She would like to possess the countess's cultural heritage and noble lineage. But the most important likeness of all, as one observer has pointed out, is that Laura commits the same error as Wanda: she nearly sends her husband out of her life.[19] In the first chapter Laura adopts her Wanda-pose, a haughty "grand manner" as her sister Page calls it; this is the first of many roles that she will play in the course of the novel (p. 11).

The opera scene, one of the plays within the play that is the novel, has multiple and important functions. Besides providing a group situation in which all the major characters are introduced, it also establishes the dichotomy between art and other kinds of experience, especially natural and commercial experience, that is crucial to the novel. The opera house is an artificial hothouse, the exact opposite of the raw wind and rain outside: "Inside it was dark, and a prolonged puff of hot air, thick with the mingled odours of flowers, perfume, upholstery, and gas, enveloped her upon the instant. It was the unmistakable, unforgettable, entrancing aroma of the theatre" (p. 16). These thick sensory effects and the extra-rich atmosphere appeal strongly to Laura. Her private palace of art, built after she marries Jadwin, reflects a similar lushness and carries the same flavor of enervating, subversive luxury. The opera house is also emblematic of

18. Quoted in Monica Stirling, *The Fine and the Wicked: The Life and Times of Ouida*, pp. 155–56.

19. Blitch, "*The Pit* and Allusive Revelations," p. 22. This study, which also interprets *The Pit* on the basis of allusions, argues quite tenably that they reveal a common egoism shared by the three main characters.

power and wealth; throngs of people wait outside to watch the millionaires come to pay homage to art. Against the world of the opera is set that of the businessmen, the wheat speculators whose daily activities are talked about while the opera is being performed. The leitmotiv of another reality, played simultaneously with the music of art, is underlined by news of a recent failure, the defeat of Helmick, an event that foreshadows Jadwin's future defeat. Representative types of both worlds, business and art, are in attendance: Jadwin, who prefers "Father, oh father, come home with me now" to opera, which he calls "fiddle-faddle, tweedle-deedle" (p. 24); and Corthell, the artist, who has seen *L'Africaine* performed in Paris.

The overwhelming importance of the opera scene is the psychological impact that the art has upon Laura. The music affects her exactly the way it does Vandover; it transports her to a sentimental heaven on earth:

> All this excitement, this world of perfume, of flowers, of exquisite costumes, of beautiful women, of fine, brave men. She looked back with immense pity to the narrow little life of her native town she had just left forever, the restricted horizon, the petty round of petty duties, the rare and barren pleasures—the library, the festival, the few concerts, the trivial plays. How easy it was to be good and noble when music such as this had become a part of one's life; how desirable was wealth when it could make possible such exquisite happiness as hers of the moment. Nobility, purity, courage, sacrifice seemed much more worth while now than a few moments ago. All things not positively unworthy became heroic, all things and all men. Landry Court was a young chevalier, pure as Galahad. Corthell was a beautiful artist-priest of the early Renaissance. Even Jadwin was a merchant prince, a great financial captain. And she herself— ah, she did not know; she dreamed of another Laura, a better, gentler, more beautiful Laura, whom everybody, everybody loved dearly and tenderly, and who loved everybody, and who should die beautifully, gently, in some garden far away—die because of a great love—beautifully, gently in the midst of flowers, die of a broken heart, and all the world should be sorry for her, and would weep over her when they found her dead and beautiful in her garden,

amid the flowers and the birds, in some far-off place, where
it was always early morning and where there was soft music.
And she was so sorry for herself, and so hurt with the
sheer strength of her longing to be good and true, and noble
and womanly, that as she sat in the front of the Cresslers'
box on that marvellous evening, the tears ran down her
cheeks again and again, and dropped upon her tight-shut,
white-gloved fingers. (pp. 17–18)

The music makes an intensely subjective impression upon
Laura. The several fantasies it invokes typify her thinking
and actions: the desire to have wealth, the sentimentaliza-
tion of herself as a cliché heroine of romance dying in a
garden, the desire to achieve ethical grandeur. The music
enables her to transcend a leaden cultural legacy, to ro-
manticize her suitors into medieval or Renaissance heroes,
and to engage in self-pity of a most delicious kind, so that
at last she weeps orgiastically. But the music is only a vehicle for Laura's subjective fantasies. Its reality is psychological; the music has no objective ethical content. Laura's
fantasies are ethically inclined because she wants a painless
and unearned moral rectitude. At another time music may
lead in the opposite direction, to the duality that Vandover
experiences in art: the duality of the spirit and the flesh.
Once, Corthell plays a portion of Liszt's *Mephisto Walzer*
and explains the meaning of the music:

> And now this movement; isn't it reckless and capricious,
> like a woman who hesitates and then takes the leap? Yet
> there's a certain nobility there, a feeling for ideals. You see it,
> of course. . . . And all the while this undercurrent of the
> sensual, and that feline, eager sentiment . . . and here, I think,
> is the best part of it, the very essence of passion, the
> voluptousness that is a veritable anguish. (p. 238)

Corthell's view of music as dualistic—possessing both the
sensual and the ideal, the voluptuous and the noble—is
more psychologically complete than Laura's one-dimension-
al sentimentalizing of music into an ethical absolute. Liszt's
composition is also totally appropriate for a seducer at work,
combining as it does idealism and sexuality.

At one point in the opera scene Laura becomes aware of

her fantasizing. Talk of business affairs—the drama of the streets—calls her attention to the commercial world of the present, which is the antithesis of a "mystic garden of some romantic dreamland" (p. 21). But the music's power is compelling; and, sparked by Corthell's declaration of love during the intermission, she merges the Laura observing the opera with the heroine of the opera:

> Ah, yes, she was loved, just as that young girl of the opera had been loved. For this one evening, at least, the beauty of life was unmarred, and no cruel word of hers should spoil it. The world was beautiful. All people were good and noble and true. To-morrow, with the material round of duties and petty responsibilities and cold, calm reason, was far, far away. (p. 22)

Here Laura knows that she is projecting an imaginary world out of the opera-induced fantasy; but, more often than not, she gets the two confused and mistakes the imaginary world of romantic art for the real world of Chicago. Her identification of her suitors with figures of romance illustrates both this tendency to prefer the past over the present and the irony of her romanticizing. Landry Court, for example, proves to be an ironical and comical Galahad, since he is the courtier who surprises the lady Laura with a kiss. Jadwin, the financial warrior-captain, also called a Napoleon, reappears in this guise many times in the novel. Though the image appeals to Laura, the fact does not, and she never pays much attention to Jadwin's exploits. Corthell, as a renaissance artist-priest (of Pre-Raphaelite precedents no doubt), comes closest to fulfilling Laura's designation. Religious imagery symbolizes his conception of art as religion, and he is endowed with oracular insight.

The opera itself has oblique connections with the action of the novel. Presented in pieces—we miss the first act, for example—the opera involves a triangle similar to that of Laura, Corthell, and Jadwin. The third act, which is described in the most detail, is especially pertinent. It is also the heroine's *grande scène*, a foreshadowing of Laura's grand manner, which climaxes in those theatrical scenes near the novel's end in which Laura successively assumes different roles, from Phèdre to Carmen, for her husband's presumed pleasure. The soprano is beseeched by two lovers (Laura has three, but the youthful Landry Court is soon out of the picture). She resists the baritone, a duke, but then falls into his arms after he forgives her for some unspecified error. Then she shifts moods and cries, "I tremble." At this point the tenor, the only one who sings in French (the others sing in Italian), enters and denounces the baritone. They duel, with the baritone the victor. The soprano seeks consolation from her confidante. In the finale the contralto (dressed as a boy) and the other principals—soprano, tenor, baritone, and basso—lament the course of events. The last act, which does not much engage Laura's attention, shows the tenor giving up the soprano and being commiserated by his friend the basso. The soprano faints once more into the arms of her confidante.

Some parallels may be noted. Jadwin is comparable to the baritone who triumphs over the tenor and forgives the soprano; Corthell, to the tenor who sings in French, is defeated once for the soprano's hand, and in the end removes himself from contention; Laura, to the soprano torn between two strong affections and addicted to histrionics; Page, Laura's sister, to the contralto who is dressed like a boy and who adumbrates the soprano's songs. In addition, Mrs. Cressler is rather like the confidante who consoles but plays no controlling part; and Aunt Wess', in her comic role, is a bit like the ludicrous chorus remarking on the central action. The ending of the opera, with the chief actors sorrowful and the heroine bereft, has slight correspondences with the novel. Laura's fantasy of herself dying in a garden is not carried out, but she does depart from a "garden" at the end and appropriately quotes the closing lines of *Paradise Lost*. Moreover, the mournful tone of loss and frustrated love does have some similarity with the end of *The Pit*, where Mr. Cressler has committed suicide, Jadwin has lost his fortune, Corthell has retreated to Europe, and Laura has forsaken a rich private aesthetic experience for the bleakness of a life largely without sensuous possibilities.

In looking at these rather weighty parallels, we should not overlook certain farcical overtones in the presentation of the opera. The singers perform in both French and Italian; but, as Joseph Katz has discovered, this seeming incongruity is in fact the result of Norris's conflation of two extant texts of the opera *Faust*, one of which was in Italian and the other in French.[20] It was also not unusual at this time for a singer to perform in either French or Italian, depending upon which language he was most comfortable with, and regardless of whether the rest of the company was singing in the same language. (Incidentally, this appears to be the same opera described in *Vandover and the Brute*.) The whole scene is richly comic and undercuts Laura's passionate ennoblement as well as her pretentions to sophistication. Significantly, Corthell is not moved to transports of ecstasy by this performance.

Although the opera is a "music-drama of passion and romance," it is not the only drama, as Laura comes to realize (p. 30). The commercial district through which Laura is driven after the opera prompts her to imagine another kind of drama: "That other drama, that other tragedy, working on there furiously, fiercely through the night, while she and all those others had sat there in that atmosphere of flowers and perfume, listening to music" (p. 36). In another passage the juxtaposition of opposite forms of drama is made even sharper:

> Yes, here was drama in deadly earnest—drama and tragedy and death, and the jar of mortal fighting. And the echoes of it invaded the very sanctuary of art, and cut athwart the music of Italy and the cadence of polite conversation, and the shock of it endured when all the world should have slept, and galvanized into vivid life all those sombre piles of office buildings. (p. 36)

20. I am grateful to Joseph Katz for sharing this information with me.

Here Laura's perception is acute. She sees, typically in dramatic metaphors, a reality different from that expressed by the opera house and the opera. Yet her apprehension is solely intellectual; this "drama" does not enlist her feelings and emotions as forcefully as does the musical drama.

The closing image of chapter 1 is of the board of trade building:

> And this was her last impression of the evening. The lighted office buildings, the murk of rain, the haze of light in the heavens, and raised against it the pile of the Board of Trade Building, black, grave, monolithic, crouching on its foundations, like a monstrous sphinx with blind eyes, silent, grave,—crouching there without a sound, without sign of life under the night and the drifting veil of rain. (p. 37)

Unlike the opera house, many meanings of which have already been divulged at this point in the novel, the board of trade building is inscrutable. Its sphinxlike intimations are not here disclosed. Still, tentative judgments are possible. This building has a sort of solid, primordial ("monolithic") reality that seems to be the opposite of the opera house. It is also more open to the elements, to the night and the rain. Yet it is more threatening (though the opera house is dangerous as well); its blackness, the satanic sign in this novel, is pure black, not dim like the "sanctuary" of the opera house. What counts most here is Laura's perception of the commercial building. To her, the board of trade is indecipherable. Her failure to understand its meaning is a significant shortcoming. If art is to be more than a private luxury, the board of trade presents a major aesthetic challenge. Laura, as we shall see, never develops an aesthetic view comprehensive enough to embrace the opera *and* the board of trade.

The next theater scene in the novel occurs in chapter 4. Like the opera, it is an integral part of the controlling structural device, the dramatic analogy. The occasion is a rehearsal for a benefit play for a children's hospital. The rehearsal is a comic disaster because of Isabel Gretry's ineptness and the director's pretensions. But the farce (of the rehearsal, for the play is apparently a melodrama) comments directly on a principal theme, the relationship between art and "reality." Monsieur Gerardy, the director and significantly a Frenchman, tells the stricken Gretry girl, who has been embarrassed into a nosebleed: "You ought to understand at last, that when one rehearses for a play one does not have the nose-bleed. It is not decent" (p. 113). Monsieur Gerardy conceives of art as a realm separate from the real world, exactly as Laura romanticizes the opera. At this rehearsal Laura adopts the grand manner out of anger at the director's rudeness to the girl. At a second rehearsal the grand manner fits perfectly Laura's role in the play as a "high-born gentlewoman visiting the home of a dependent" (p. 124). This scene ends as the opera one does, with the players and spectators departing into the rain, into another order of reality.

The characterization of Laura in scenes outside the theater or the opera house draws heavily upon dramatic analogy as well. Indeed, Laura's problem is that she carries acting into her private life and fails to be sincere and honest as a result. Norris's idea of the proper divorcement of acting from private life can be seen in an interview with actress Isabel Irving in 1896. She impressed Norris with her sincerity:

> There is not the least pose about Miss Irving in her private life. Her acting ceases the moment she leaves the stage. . . . In other words, she does not act the role of a celebrity—she prefers, which is far more pleasing, to be herself simply, frankly, without the slightest affectation.[21]

Laura, on the other hand, is constantly affecting a manner and assuming a pose. She has a "tragic shadow" (p. 156). Moreover, she consciously conceives of herself as an actress and of her marriage as a chance to play a role. She explains love itself with a dramatic image drawn from the courtly-love tradition: "And it's her part, if she likes, to be cold and distant" (p. 159). She accurately predicts her life with

21. "Trilby and Princess Flavia: An Interviewer, Two Actresses, and Several Confidences."

Jadwin as a role: "Think of it, that beautiful house, and servants, and carriages, and paintings, and, oh, honey, how I will dress the part!" (p. 161).

Laura's name is a clue to the courtly-love mythology that provides a model for her and her circle of lovers. From Petrarch on, the name *Laura* has been associated with romantic lovers and courtly ladies. Her maiden name, *Dearborn*, is appropriate too. On the denotative level it fits nicely with the aristocratic associations of *Laura*; and on the historical, it connects Laura, who is in partial revolt against New England puritanism, with the West, with Fort Dearborn, the early United States military post (1803–1837) that became Chicago. The names of her suitors are apposite too. As Walter John Bauer has observed, all three have the word *court* in their names: Court, Curtis, Corthell.[22]

The implications of Laura's posing and role playing are numerous and severe. After three years of marriage she has become almost completely a theatrical persona rather than a person:

> The untrained, unguided instinct of the actress in Laura had fostered in her a curious penchant toward melodrama. She had a taste for the magnificent. She revelled in these great musical "effects" upon her organ, the grandiose easily appealed to her, while as for herself, the rôle of the *grande dame*, with this wonderful house for background and environment, came to be for her, quite unconsciously, a sort of game in which she delighted.
>
> It was by this means that, in the end, she succeeded in fitting herself to her new surroundings. Innocently enough, and with a harmless, almost childlike, affectation, she posed a little, and by so doing found the solution of the incongruity between herself—the Laura of moderate means and quiet life—and the massive luxury with which she was now surrounded. Without knowing it, she began to act the part of a great lady—and she acted it well. She assumed the existence of her numerous servants as she assumed the fact of the trees in the park; she gave herself into the hands of her maid, not as Laura Jadwin of herself would have

22. "The Man-Woman Relationship in the Novels of Frank Norris," p. 249.

> done it, clumsily and with the constraint of inexperience,
> but as she would have done it if she had been acting the
> part on the stage, with an air, with all the nonchalance of a
> marquise, with—in fine—all the superb condesension of
> her "grand manner." (p. 202)

Fulfilling the role she played in Monsieur Gerardy's melodrama, Laura has allowed her grand manner, which predates
her coming to Chicago, to become her only manner. The
consequences are solitude, a nervousness approaching the
neurotic, loneliness, and above all a lack of self-knowledge.

Role playing is a threat to sincerity and honesty, a self-
deception that can lead to the loss of a consistent and true
identity. With Corthell in her rooms, Laura sentimentalizes
her past, inventing a past that the reader has trouble be-
lieving because there is plenty of contradictory evidence
pointing to its falsity: "Ah, I was happy in those days—just
a freckled, black-haired slip of a little girl, with my frock
torn and my hands all scratched with the berry bushes"
(p. 281). This self-portrait is straight out of popular romance. Reinvoking the image a bit later, she sees her father
as "Squire Dearborn," a sure clue that the source of her
fantasy is some English fiction, or worse, some American
version of English fiction (p. 282). Further, Laura allows
the self-dramatization to confuse her to the point where she
cannot tell gesture from substance, role from identity:

> She had begun by dramatizing, but by now she was acting
> —acting with all her histrionic power at fullest stretch,
> acting the part of a woman unhappy amid luxuries, who
> looked back with regret and with longing toward a joyous,
> simple childhood. She was sincere and she was not sincere.
> (p. 281)

Laura is the playwright of her own character, and with every
role she takes on she insulates herself a bit more from the
order of reality represented by the real-life drama on the
night of the opera.

Her role playing has an explicitly demonic side as well.
The grand manner is linked with sensuality:

But at moments such as this she knew that there was another Laura Jadwin—the Laura Jadwin who might have been a great actress, who had a "temperament," who was impulsive. This was the Laura of the "grand manner," who played the rôle of the great lady from room to room of her vast house, who read Meredith, who revelled in swift gallops through the park on jet-black, long-tailed horses, who affected black velvet, black jet, and black lace in her gowns, who was conscious and proud of her pale, stately beauty—the Laura Jadwin, in fine, who delighted to recline in a long chair in the dim, beautiful picture gallery and listen with half-shut eyes to the great golden organ thrilling to the passion of Beethoven and Liszt. (pp. 239–40)

Acting, blackness, sexual energy, and music merge here to form the same kind of link between art and sensuousness that occurs in *Vandover*. Corthell is a dangerous cicerone for Laura, who never knows or learns how to understand aesthetic experience. As strongly as *Vandover*, this novel depicts a character who is split between one conception of art as spiritual and uplifting and another of art as sensuous and destructive.

Laura's aesthetic sensibility is defined with reference to other kinds of art besides drama. Her background, her experience in Chicago, and her tutelage by Corthell constitute the principal subject of the novel, paralleling if not overshadowing Jadwin's commercial activities. Interestingly, the direction of Laura's cultural enrichment is the opposite of that in *The Octopus*; she moves from a culturally barren East to the raw commercial city of Chicago, where art is booming. Laura's New England is a dismal place:

It was picturesque, but lamentably narrow. The life was barren, the "New England spirit" prevailed in all its severity; and this spirit seemed to her a veritable cult, a sort of religion, wherein the Old Maid was the priestess, the Spinster the officiating devotee, the thing worshipped the Great Unbeautiful, and the ritual unremitting, unrelenting Housework. (p. 40)

The worship of the "Great Unbeautiful" is replaced by worship of the beautiful, under the direction of the artist-priest

Corthell. Even in bleak New England, however, Laura had managed to cultivate some awareness of art. She attended the exotic Episcopalian church and once saw two plays in Boston (*Marie Stuart* and *Macbeth*, one of her roles after her marriage is Lady Macbeth). The Boston adventure aroused her theatrical ambitions and brought a visit from a group of concerned Presbyterians.

As a young girl she had also cultivated a taste for literature to the point of its becoming an "actual passion" (p. 38). Under the guidance of a private tutor, she read Shakespeare, Racine (whom she can still quote from the French), Tennyson and the Victorian poets, the New England poets and essayists, and, as a concession to the modern, Howells. Her motive for reading becomes clear in a conversation with Landry Court. The object of praise is *Wanda*:

> "You can say what you like, but it's beautiful—a beautiful love story—and it does tell about noble, unselfish people. I suppose it has its faults, but it makes you feel better for reading it, and that's what all your *Wreckers* in the world would never do." (p. 51)

Her preference for Ouida over Stevenson results from pernicious tastes: the desire for an idealized love story and an upbeat moral.[23] Such artistic values mislead her when she measures these unreal and sentimental people with the actuality of Jadwin and herself: "I thought when love came it was to be—oh, uplifting, something glorious like Juliet's love or Marguerite's" (p. 153). Mrs. Cressler offers a useful corrective view: "Oh, that's what you read about in trashy novels, . . . or the kind you see at the matinées" (p. 153). Jadwin's view of novels both supports and criticizes Laura's. His belief in art's ethical purpose mirrors hers:

23. In one of Norris's critical essays Ouida is used, along with other best-selling authors of the day, as a kind of minimal standard by which to gauge the American reader, the point being that it is better to read the "Duchesses and Ouida and Edna Lyalls and Albert Rosses" than to read nothing at all. "The American Public and 'Popular' Fiction," in *The Literary Criticism of Frank Norris*, ed. Donald Pizer, p. 128.

"But I believe that any art that don't make the world better and happier is no art at all, and is only fit for the dump heap" (p. 205). Ironically, Laura tries to improve Jadwin's taste in fiction. She reads Meredith to him, whom he cannot stomach; he prefers instead Jules Verne or the popular novels of Archibald Clavering Gunter, *Mr. Potter of Texas* and *Mr. Barnes of New York*.[24] But one writer she introduces him to—Howells—he likes immensely. He knows Howells's characters, he says, and in an obvious self-reflexive context he champions Lapham over Bromfield Cory, that "dilletanty" (p. 205).

Laura's relationship with Corthell, a dilettante himself, is the most important influence on her imitative, fourth-rate, and faddish artistic opinions. Under his guidance she participates in a crash program to improve her tastes. She stops reading novels, turning instead to "solemn works full of allusions to 'Man' and 'Destiny' "; studies French; attends music concerts; and spends one afternoon a week listening to Corthell read aloud from Keats, Browning, and Edwin Arnold (p. 105). Later, Laura backslides to reading novels, no doubt the kind that Corthell thinks will eventually disappear, the love story. Laura is, however, a more steadfast disciple with regard to music and painting. Corthell reveals a new world to her in both arts. In a key scene in chapter 7 he plays a variety of compositions on Jadwin's organ. His ostensible aim is to improve her tastes; his real one, to seduce her. He plays Mendelssohn's *Consolation*; Beethoven's *Appasionata*, the F Minor Sonata; and Liszt's *Mephisto Walzer*. Laura's predisposition to be seductively swayed by music has already been established in the first chapter, and Corthell's belief that it is the most "intimate" of the arts points to his deliberate manipulation of the music to serve his own sensuous needs (p. 240).

Corthell's performance stirs Laura emotionally, just as the music at the opera did. She recants all her previous tastes:

24. Gunter was a San Francisco author, too, and a member of the Bohemian Club.

Laura was transfixed, all but transported. Here was something better than Gounod and Verdi, something above and
beyond the obvious one, two, three, one, two, three of the
opera scores as she knew them and played them. . . .

She felt all at once as though a whole new world were
opened to her. She stood on Pisgah. And she was ashamed
and confused at her ignorance of those things which Corthell
tactfully assumed that she knew as a matter of course. . . .
Ah, but she would make amends now. No more Verdi and
Bougereau [sic]. She would get rid of the Bathing Nymphs.
Never, never again would she play the "Anvil Chorus."
Corthell should select her pictures, and should play to her
from Liszt and Beethoven that music which evoked all the
turbulent emotion, all the impetuosity and fire and exaltation
that she felt was hers. (pp. 238–39)

The level of Laura's discarded tastes is well summed up in the
artists cited here. Hers is a middlebrow awareness of music
and art. Gounod's characteristic sentimentality and vague
religiosity fuel her ethical posturing, and the "Anvil Chorus"
from Verdi's *Il Trovatore* is as hackneyed as any of Jadwin's
favorite songs.[25] Besides reflecting Laura's trite taste, this
scene shows once again the subjective power of music to
stimulate emotions and feelings in Norris's characters. Further, there is her mistaken attribution of some kind of ethical
correctness to forms of art. Introduced to a better art, she is
eager to "make amends" for her former sins. Carrying out
the art-as-religion imagery, Corthell is a Moses figure leading Laura to Pisgah. Norris's satire of middle-class artistic
pretensions could hardly be sharper.

Corthell's superior knowledge of painting causes Laura
to abandon Bouguereau just as she does Gounod and Verdi.
Her favorite painting is a Bouguereau of "nymphs bathing in
a woodland pool" (p. 188), until Corthell demolishes her
judgment by noting that the work is facile and without substance: "For all there is *in* his picture—back of it—a fine
hanging, a beautiful vase would have exactly the same value

25. It was a standard piece, for example, at the Orpheum, San
Francisco's leading vaudeville theater. *Orpheum Programme*, 8 June
1896.

upon your wall" (p. 236). One critic believes that because Corthell is an aesthete "who has removed himself from the world," his view of Bouguereau, who was Norris's teacher in Paris, cannot be taken to reflect Norris's opinion.[26] That Norris held a similarly low opinion of Bouguereau's work, though, is evident from a satirical sketch that he wrote in 1896, wherein he defines a student's mediocre ability by saying, "Bouguereau is his enthusiasm; he can rise no higher than that."[27] Corthell prefers instead another painting hanging in her gallery, one to which Laura has paid little attention. It is a landscape by an unknown Western artist, and Corthell's explication of its meaning is worth attention. The painting depicts a little pool at twilight; the dominant mood is "gloom and . . . sadness" (p. 236); and the pool itself, Corthell interprets as an unfathomable heart that bespeaks despair. Corthell may be, as one critic thinks, talking about Laura's "heart of unplumbed depths,"[28] but he is certainly expressing a sensitivity to art that is more impressive than Laura's received canon of acceptable and known artists. This kind of insight on Cothell's part, plus other examples, as we shall see, adds to the complexity of his characterization and makes the description of him as merely a dilettante unsatisfactory.

Nothing exposes Laura's cultural pretensions more than the subplot of Page Dearborn and Landry Court, whose characters echo and satirize the main plot of Laura's and Jadwin's aesthetic contretemps. Of all the subplots in Norris's fiction, this is his masterpiece. The Page-Court romance is a witty, satirical, and enlightening commentary on Laura's character. Page, Laura's younger sister, is to some degree a double, with the major difference being that Page has no grand manner and therefore suffers no emotional split between role playing and her "real" self. Page's main aesthetic

26. William B. Dillingham, *Frank Norris: Instinct and Art*, p. 160n.
27. "Western Types: An Art Student."
28. Bauer, "The Man-Woman Relationship in the Novels of Frank Norris," p. 266.

interest is literature, and her view of writing is as sentimental and romantic as Laura's. She keeps a journal filled with effusions that inadvertently parody Laura's ethical fantasies:

> "I got my journal and wrote down, 'Yet in a few days,
> and thee, the all-beholding sun shall see no more.' It's from
> Thanatopsis, you know, and I thought how beautiful it
> would be to leave all this world, and soar and soar, right up
> to higher planes and be at peace." (p. 158)

Both the quoting from a well-known poet (one of Laura's New England pantheon) and the idealized sentiment are exactly like Laura's penchant for weepy dreaming. Another journal entry is a very funny parody of Laura's outpourings on the necessity of love and of her habit of turning to literature for an authoritative source:

> A world without love—oh, what an awful thing that would
> be. Oh, love is so beautiful—so beautiful, that it makes me
> sad. When I think of love in all its beauty I am sad, sad
> like Romola in George Eliot's well-known novel of the
> same name. (p. 160)

Page's journal also expresses a belief in abstract ethical ideals and allows for a partially sublimated emotional release; thus, it precisely mirrors Laura's combined ethical and erotic stimulations:

> She filled page after page with "impressions," "outpourings,"
> queer little speculations about her soul, quotations from
> poets, solemn criticisms of new novels, or as often as not
> mere purposeless meanderings of words, exclamatory,
> rhapsodic—involved lucubrations quite meaningless and
> futile, but which at times she re-read with vague thrills of
> emotion and mystery. (p. 157)

The courtship of Landry and Page echoes that of Jadwin and Laura, and even more satirically, that of Landry and Laura. In fact, Landry tells both sisters how much it means to have a woman understand a man. One of his evening conversations with Page duplicates a similar discussion with Laura; in both cases the girls argue on behalf of uplifting authors such as Ouida and Charles Lamb, while Landry defends modern authors such as Howells. Page's ideas about love are just as unrealistic as Laura's and stem from the same source, idealistic literature. Thus she tells Landry of her notion of self-sacrifice as the highest expression of love, citing Enoch Arden as her model. Landry debunks this Tennysonian ideal, though he lets himself come under Page's influence, vowing comically to pursue high culture for her sake: "I'll get that *Stones of Venice* I've heard you speak of, and I'll sit up nights—and keep awake with black coffee— but I'll read that book from cover to cover" (p. 211). Page later explains to Laura that Landry wants to be more than a "mere money-getting machine" and that together they are going to read *The Ring and the Book* (p. 214).

The last glimpse we have of Page and Landry is a fine comic summary of Laura's cultural pretensions. Page writes her sister from New York:

> We are reading George Sand out loud, and are making up the longest vocabulary. To-night we are going to a concert, and I've found out that there's a really fine course of lectures to be given soon on "Literary Tendencies," or something like that. *Quel chance.* Landry is intensely interested. You've no idea what a deep mind he has, Laura—a real thinker. (p. 398)

Here Page's activities are a checklist of Laura's cultural campaign: reading a fashionable French author, vocabulary building (once Laura rushes home to look up *pergola* after having pretended to Corthell that she understood the word), attending lectures, quoting French, trying to feed culture to a commercial man. This subplot stresses the first of the three possible attitudes to take toward art: (1) to approach it as a trivial, fashionable, genteel undertaking, harmless but chic, a kind of philistine dilettantism; (2) to reject it, as the New England cult of the unbeautiful does; (3) to immerse oneself in it to the point of losing contact with other important human activities. None of these, it should be obvious, is adequate from Norris's viewpoint.

Norris's central device for illuminating Laura's aesthetic sensibility is to develop the age-old plot contrivance of a love triangle in terms of aesthetic opposites. Torn between two men, Laura chooses the businessman-warrior over the artist-priest, marrying Jadwin and forgoing Corthell. But after three years of marriage the triangular pattern re-emerges in a much more demonic way, for now choosing Corthell over Jadwin means adultery or divorce or both. From the beginning of the novel the rival heroes are presented in aesthetic terms. Corthell lives in the "calm, still atmosphere of art, in the cult of the beautiful" (p. 59). Jadwin, a fighter, partakes of the "Battle of the Street" and is the embodiment of romance (p. 60). Laura, a "daughter of the frontier," chooses Jadwin because, in Norris's "masculine-feminine ethic,"[29] he appeals to the *woman* in her (p. 60). The problem with Jadwin, though, is that Laura has to imagine him as interesting. As a medieval or Renaissance soldier, Jadwin appeals to Laura's romantic imagination. As himself, he is a figure without much sensuous resonance. This air of abstraction surrounds the entire characterization of Jadwin. Corthell, on the other hand, is always invested with specific, concrete, sensuous details. The effect is similar to the pattern of abstract versus concrete treatments of virtue and demonism that informs *Vandover*.

The contrasting milieus and tastes of Jadwin and Corthell—and Laura's reaction to each—confirm the pattern of abstract versus concrete imagery that is apparent in analytical passages. All we know about Jadwin's house—the one he lives in before he marries Laura—is contained in one sentence: "He lived on Michigan Avenue, near the corner of Twenty-first Street, in one of those discouraging eternal yellow limestone houses with a basement dining room" (p. 70). The bleakness of this environment is matched by Jadwin's noncommercial interests. Following the ideal of Dwight Moody, he has organized a Sunday school for orphans, a worthy but intrinsically dull enterprise, as Laura realizes when she visits there and is appalled by the platitudinous banners with mottoes, the floral decorations of

29. The phrase is from Donald Pizer's study of the three minor novels; see "The Masculine-Feminine Ethic in Frank Norris' Popular Novels."

calla lilies, the general air of poverty. Jadwin's religion is another version of the New England cult of the unbeautiful that Laura has fled; she could have had calla lilies in Barrington (barren), Mass. Jadwin's music, grinding Protestant hymns, is a stunning contrast with Corthell's Liszt and Beethoven. After the visit Laura recalls this depressing image: "And the picture he made leading the singing, beating time with the hymn-book, and between the verses declaring that 'he wanted to hear everyone's voice in the next verse,' did not appeal very forcibly to her imagination" (p. 115).

In contrast, Corthell's surroundings have a formative influence upon Laura's aesthetic sensibility. His studio, with its dim light, velvet hangings, and perfumed atmosphere, causes her to include an art gallery in the mansion Jadwin builds for her. This room, which contains an electric organ large enough for a cathedral, is a palace of art:

> It was shaped like a rotunda, and topped with a vast airy dome of coloured glass. Here and there about the room were glass cabinets full of bibelots, ivory statuettes, old snuff boxes, fans of the sixteenth and seventeenth centuries. The walls themselves were covered with a multitude of pictures, oils, water-colours, with one or two pastels. (p. 188)

The dimness, the Shelleyan effect ("a vast airy dome of coloured glass"), the religious overtones, all these qualities are characteristic of Corthell and alien to Jadwin. It is Jadwin's money, though, that paid for the gallery, and his presence is felt in the electric lights.

In his typical inventory fashion, Norris provides a full description of Corthell's apartment. It is "picturesque" and "carefully planned" and contains many "small masterpiece[s] of art or workmanship," including fine eighteenth-century books, copper-leaf walls, a Roman bust, a rare illuminated manuscript, statuettes and drawings by artists ranging from the Renaissance to moderns like Saint-Gaudens, a tapestry depicting a classical scene, and so on (pp. 272–73). The room attests to Corthell's arcane and eclectic tastes; items appear in this decor that are not found elsewhere in Norris's fiction. Most importantly, every object in Corthell's house is *his*: the setting is an expression of his sensibility. On the contrary, Jadwin hires decorators to furnish his house. The result is an impersonal background, a mechanical effect quite different from the handcrafted and highly individual style of Corthell's room:

> There was nothing to offend, and much to delight in the results they obtained in the dining room, breakfast room, parlours, drawing rooms, and suites of bedrooms. But Laura, though the beauty of it all enchanted her, could never rid herself of a feeling that it was not hers. It impressed her with its splendour of natural woods and dull "colour effects," its cunning electrical devices, its mechanical contrivances for comfort, like the ready-made luxury and "convenience" of a Pullman. (p. 200)

Of course the room does not express Laura's personality; it expresses Jadwin's. He plays the organ with a mechanical attachment, a practice that Corthell finds unspeakably gauche. Jadwin is symbolized by electric lights; Corthell, by cathedral dimness. Jadwin is a man of the dynamo age; Corthell, of the virgin. It is Corthell, of course, who speaks derisively of the "decadence of American industrial arts" (p. 52).

Laura's rooms are expressions of her "individuality" and of Corthell's aesthetic mode. Personal, arty, and traditional, they contain skin rugs, books, plants, and give the effect of a "wide, airy place" (p. 279). From the gallery, to her private rooms, the influence of Corthell is quite strong; and Laura increasingly adjusts her life to his (after Jadwin, becoming absorbed in his business, has begun to remove himself from her presence).

Laura is caught, then, between two opposite types of men. Jadwin is so intrinsically dull, his apprehension so sterile, his ideas so cliché ridden and conventional that, to make him interesting at all, Laura has to invent another Jadwin, a warrior engaged in mighty battles and holding the fates of nations in his hands. That his actions bear out this imagery is not to the point, since Laura never knows or

cares to know this side of his life. The most telling remark
by Jadwin in the novel is his observation to Corthell after
having made a killing on the market: "It takes it out of you,
Mr. Corthell, to make five hundred thousand in about ten
hours" (p. 242). What it takes out is the capacity or desire
to appreciate art. Corthell possesses a rich aesthetic sensibility, Jadwin almost none. Norris's theme, that the commercial life exhausts the possibilities for a rich private
existence, has been justly praised.[30] Still, it is Jadwin and the
rejection of aesthetic experience that Laura chooses at the
novel's end. Jadwin, who spurns the "pictures, the heavy
hangings, the glass cabinets of bibelots" (p. 300), offers a
life not far removed from that Presbyterian contempt for
the sensuous world that Laura had found so oppressive in
her New England days. Laura's statement to Jadwin explains
why she prefers him: "Oh, you are a man, Curtis; a great,
strong, kind-hearted man, with no little graces, nor petty
culture, nor trivial fine speeches, nor false sham, imitation
polish" (p. 300). If Laura's description of the aesthete refers
to Corthell, as it must, since she knows no other, it is unsatisfactory and denies her own experience of having taken
legitimate pleasure in art and in Corthell's sensuous world.

The description is stereotypical and may fit other artists
in Norris's fiction, Hartrath in *The Octopus* for example,
but not Corthell, who is a far more complex and finally
ambiguous character than has been previously granted.[31]

30. Ziff has formulated this point beautifully: "Thus the vital
tension of the novel is not between the bulls and bears in the pit—
as Norris frequently seems to claim it is—but between the pit and
the opera; between a masculinity that is vital but totally spends itself
in business, leaving only a husk of a man for private life, and a masculinity suspected by society because it possesses the characteristics
conventionally associated with women but which leads to a rich
private life even though it does nothing to build up the country"
(*The American 1890s: Life and Times of a Lost Generation*, pp.
270–71).

31. Pizer, for example, notes only the uplift side of Corthell: "He
is associated in Laura's mind with Art and with a high but formalized
passion—in other words, with the opera itself—and he appeals to
this side of her nature" (*The Novels of Frank Norris*, p. 171). Ernest

Corthell is Norris's most rounded and successful portrait of the aesthete, possessing all the necessary attributes: a devotion to beauty, especially of the arcane and sophisticated kind; a remoteness from the ordinary affairs of men; a penchant for elegant discourse; a personal fastidiousness; a hedonism with just the slightest trace of decadence; a feminine sensibility. Jadwin sums up the stereotyped figure of the aesthete as it existed (and exists) in the popular mind:

> "But I don't believe they [women] were made—any more than Christ was—to cultivate—beyond a certain point—their own souls, and refine their own minds, and live in a sort of warmed-over, dilettante, stained-glass world of seclusion and exclusion." (p. 118)

Jadwin must have Corthell, his arch rival for Laura, in mind here. Certainly part of Corthell's life embodies the ideas that Jadwin scorns. When Laura meets the artist accidentally, three years after her marriage, she learns of his recent activities. He has been in Tuscany amid "gardens and marble pergolas" (p. 228) and has been spending his time "merely idling, and painting a little, and studying some thirteenth-century glass in Avignon and Siena" (p. 230).

If this were all Corthell is, a connoisseur of stained glass and a devotee of gardens, the charges of seclusiveness and exclusiveness might be warranted. But the fact is that Norris grants Corthell a power of vision and insight into modern life—Jadwin's sphere—that makes Corthell seem much less insulated and narcissistic than otherwise would be the case. Periodically he returns to Chicago for "a touch of our hard, harsh city again" (p. 228). In a conversation with Laura he amends her criticism of Jadwin as a man too absorbed in his business to a general criticism of the danger of becoming totally absorbed in any activity, including art and religion. Developing this point further, he argues that each person's true worth should be measured by his contribution to the

---

Marchand includes Corthell with Norris's other portraits of stereotypical aesthetes (*Frank Norris, A Study*, p. 140).

general welfare. He concludes by offering a social ethic that is the very opposite of a view founded upon merely personal relationships and private worlds: "A little good contributed by everybody to the race is of more, infinitely more, importance than a great deal of good contributed by one individual to another" (p. 234). Laura takes up the argument and makes two further assumptions: that the type, not the individual, matters; and that the type will not be allowed to deteriorate, supported as it is by God and nature, which are the same. She finds this reasoning "beautiful" (p. 235), and her facile accession is as important as the idea that is being advanced. Corthell's espousal of Lecontian altruism[32] (a connecting link with *The Octopus*) is hardly a sign of Norris's disapproval. Intellectually, Corthell manages to embrace modern life, even to interpret it. Aesthetically, however, he remains, with a few exceptions such as the Western painting, committed to stained-glass art.

Corthell, then, cannot be pigeonholed as a dilettante, as a sham like Hartrath in *The Octopus*, or as an effete third-rater like the aesthetes in Norris's criticism and in the short story "Dying Fires." He is not euphemistically homosexual either, and of all Norris's artists (excluding that would-be artist Vandover) Corthell is the only one who actively pursues a woman rather than just hanging around. Measured against Jadwin's force and vigor, however, Corthell's masculinity pales; but, and this is the point, he is granted some masculinity, a feature typically denied the artist in Norris's world.

Psychologically, Corthell radiates a great fund of sexuality. It is this aura, the psychological effect of his presence upon Laura, that in fact makes Corthell seem a much more dangerous sexual entity than Jadwin, whose sexuality resides in personal directness and force but, most of the time, because he is absent so much, has to be embellished by Laura's fantasizing. Jadwin is more convincingly a bull at

32. Pizer thinks, though, that Corthell's position regarding "the universal benevolence of racial evolution" is "too abstract and too brief, and . . . not pursued" (*The Novels of Frank Norris*, p. 175).

the stock market than he is at home. Corthell's erotic effect upon Laura informs several analytical passages. He makes her self-conscious of her sex and touches her impulses: "But Corthell seemed able to reach all that was impetuous, all that was unreasoned in her nature" (p. 128). "Why was it that from the very first hours of her acquaintance with this man, and in every circumstance of their intimacy, she had always acted upon impulse? What was there in him that called into being all that was reckless in her?" (pp. 343–44). *Impulse* is the key word; to the puritan imagination Corthell the artist symbolizes abandoning conventional restraint and yielding to passion. Corthell opens the way to Laura's darkest self, as one passage makes explicit: "Her troubles were multiplying; she, too, was in the current, the end of which was a pit—a pit black and without bottom" (p. 345).

The resolution of Laura's crisis is achieved through two major theatrical scenes that bring together the twin themes of the novel as play and Laura as actor. On each occasion Laura assumes a variety of famous roles, each of which provides allusive commentary on her dilemma. In the first instance she carries to ludicrous heights those melodramatic tendencies inherent in the "grand manner" style. Thus she assumes the guise of famous heroines in an effort to express feelings that she does not herself understand:

> "This great house, all the beauty of it, and all this wealth, what does it amount to?" Her voice was the voice of Phèdre, and the gesture of lassitude with which she let her arms fall into her lap was precisely that which only the day before she had used to accompany Portia's plaint of
> "—my little body is a-weary of this great world."
> Yet, at the same time, Laura knew that her heart was genuinely aching with real sadness, and that the tears which stood in her eyes were as sincere as any she had ever shed. (pp. 281–82)

The allusion to Phèdre illuminates Laura's potential for self-destruction; each woman becomes infatuated with another man in her husband's absence. The allusion to Portia appropriately recalls another Laura, the sentimental girl who in the opera scene delightfully imagines her own death. This is one of several Shakespearean allusions in the novel. At other times Laura compares herself to Juliet in a self-indulgent, sentimental way and to Lady Macbeth, an ironic comparison in that Laura does not recognize the cruel affinity that she shares with this woman capable of ruthlessly disposing of her husband.

Laura's roles here are a form of self-alienation; she blends her feelings into gestures appropriate to Phèdre and Portia but has no gestures appropriate to Laura. She is a heroine of melodrama who cannot be her natural self. What is that self? Jadwin thinks that he knows, as he tells Laura after her frantic performance: "It's sort of overwrought—a little, and unnatural. I like you best when you are your old self, quiet, and calm, and dignified. It's when you are quiet that you are at your best. I didn't know you had this streak in you" (p. 298). But the problem is that Laura is not merely the person described by Jadwin. While there is from the beginning a quiet, restrained, housewifely Laura, there is also, from the beginning, an emotional, unconventional, deeply passionate Laura who finds inadequate and often absurd expression through her dramatic personae and her contact with Corthell and art. Such roles are unnatural in Jadwin's view because they belong to another sphere, to the decadent, immoral, and destructive world of antibourgeois culture; moreover, they signify and dramatize a passion that is too natural—and too dangerous—to countenance. As in *Vandover*, the alliance of art with passion is what makes it suspect.

Laura's climactic theatrical performance occurs in the next-to-last chapter. It is her birthday, and she expects to regain the attention of Jadwin. She therefore prepares very carefully for the event:

> She disdained a "costume" on this great evening. It was not to be "Théodora" now, nor "Juliet," nor "Carmen." It was to be only Laura Jadwin—just herself, unaided by theatricals, unadorned by tinsel. But it seemed consistent none the less to choose her most beautiful gown for the occasion, to

panoply herself in every charm that was her own. Her dress,
that closely sheathed the low, flat curves of her body and
that left her slender arms and neck bare, was one shimmer
of black scales, iridescent, undulating with light to her every
movement. In the coils and masses of her black hair she
fixed her two great *cabochons* of pearls, and clasped about
her neck her palm-broad collaret of pearls and diamonds.
Against one shoulder nodded a bunch of Jacqueminots,
royal red, imperial. (p. 386)

By rejecting such roles as Carmen, who is an irresponsible
and supremely selfish woman, Laura indicates her desire to
be what Jadwin wants, a dutiful wife. Even so, in this scene
she is still playing a role. Her noncostume is of course a
costume, a strategy, simply her old grand-manner self with
embellishments—rather sinister ones—borrowed from Corthell. Instead of the American Beauty roses that she wore
in her first appearance in the novel, she has on Jacqueminots, which are suggestive of Corthell's French influence
and, through the secondary allusion to the French general's
name, of conquest. Her dress and hair have ophidian overtones: "shimmer of black scales," "undulating," "coils."
She is both serpent and, as she imagines herself at the height
of her exultation over her coming victory, Eve (p. 387). In
a moment of real insight, however, she realizes that this
Laura, too, is a persona, a theatrical creation; and she labels
her present role as "this display of her beauty, this parade
of dress, this exploitation of self" (p. 388).

When Jadwin fails to arrive home on time, Laura fran-
tically turns to Corthell, who has remembered her birthday.
Vacillating, angry at the artist for his lack of assertiveness,
Laura nonetheless declares her love for him, only to collapse
into her husband's arms upon his sudden appearance. The
inattentive reader may well miss the point. Laura, who has
committed adultery with Corthell, is now renouncing that
dangerous passion in favor of a renewed commitment to her
husband. As Joseph Katz has demonstrated, Norris's presentation of the adultery scene in chapter 8 subtly exploits
a "bounty of literary, musical, pictorial, and mythological
symbols" to set up the "erotic context in which everything

else is to be interpreted."[33] Here, in the aftermath of that adultery, the imagery confirms a different Eve from the one Laura imagined herself to be. She and Jadwin are two fallen, sinful creatures: "Pressed close together, Curtis Jadwin and his wife sat there in the vast, gorgeous room, silent and trembling, ridden with unnamed fears, groping in the darkness" (p. 395).

The way to escape the darkness brought on by the lures of art and impulse is to leave the sensuous world behind, to go out of the garden. Laura quotes from *Paradise Lost* at the novel's end, as she and her husband leave for the West. Her newest role is dual: she is a nurse and a helpmate, neither of which has anything to do with aesthetic experience, and neither of which is very far at all from Barrington, Mass., Dwight Moody, and the cult of the unbeautiful.[34] Aesthetic privation seems preferable to aesthetic experience. The new Jadwins sell their books and art objects and gladly leave the palace of art, the now "denuded rooms" (p. 401).[35]

Laura's hair symbolizes the movement toward denial of sensuous experience. In the opening scene her hair is black, thick, and richly vital; it suggests both sexual power and portentous drama. Later, under the stress of courtship, it becomes a sign of self-absorption and nervousness; she does not like for anyone to touch it. In the climactic scene her hair is again evocative of sensuality, and threateningly so. At the end, though, the hair is very carefully under control, ma-

33. "Eroticism in American Literary Realism," p. 46. In a masterful explication Katz explains the sexual implications of a heart-shaped matchbox, traces the connections between the opera *Faust* and the lovers Corthell and Laura, and shows that Jadwin suffers headache pains conventionally associated with the horns of cuckoldry (p. 48).

34. Two other Norris heroines choose nursing for a vocation: Blix (*Blix*) and Lloyd Searight (*A Man's Woman*).

35. Ziff has remarked perceptively on the unhappy overtones of the ending: "Laura has Jadwin again, but he is drained of the virility which attracted her; he has her again, but she will no longer indulge the tastes which contributed to her glamour. They are a pair of broken people who could not satisfy each other when each pursued his own bent, but who lost their charm and interest in the sacrifices they must make to mutual accommodation" (*The American 1890s: Life and Times of a Lost Generation*, p. 273).

tronly, the hair of a nurse. When Jadwin asks her whatever became of Corthell, the unspoken answer is: "Laura settled a comb in the back of her hair" (p. 400). Her spoken answer is, "You remember—I told you—told you all about it" (p. 400). Jadwin remembers, but without rancor, and the couple are ready to put the past behind them.

The last image in *The Pit* is of the board of trade building. The language is virtually identical to that at the close of chapter 1. Now, as after the opera, Laura is unable to read the building's meaning, which is hidden by the "veil of rain" (p. 403). Her exclusive aesthetic, fostered by Corthell's cloistered art, has ignored such realities as the board of trade building. Similarly, Jadwin, a board of trade man, at this moment intently reading a railroad schedule, has ignored the aesthetic possibilities of Corthell's world. Neither Laura nor Jadwin possesses a large enough perspective, an aesthetic view comprehensive enough to contain both worlds. At the end husband and wife are in alignment, but at a depressing cost; they have had to deny aesthetic and sensuous experience. And Corthell is among the stained-glass relics of the European past. A true aesthetic, which no one in the novel attains, should be able to embrace the sphinxlike board of trade building and the palaces of *haute culture*, whether they are opera houses or private mansions.

The Briefest of Afterwords

If I have succeeded in altering the image of Norris as a slow-moving beast slouching from the gutters of Zola's Paris or as a slapdash kid novelist on the make, then perhaps a start has been made toward seeing him as his contemporaries did, as a "writer who was considered unique in his own time."[1] This new image of Norris as aesthetic critic and skillful architect of fiction is not, however, the only possible image of Norris; nor should it be. He was protean and astonished his contemporaries with his swift passage from one genre to another, from *Blix* to *McTeague*. But it is a Norris whom we need to recognize and appreciate, and it is essentially the Norris that W. D. Howells saw and rated ahead of Stephen Crane. Judging by Howells's eulogy for Norris in 1902, Norris seems to have been the heir apparent, the creater of work "so vast in scope while so fine and beautiful in detail."[2] By way of closing, it is interesting to remember that Norris had called the Howells tradition in American fiction the only truly American tradition; but it is even more interesting to remember how he said it. How he said it is the fundamental Norris, for me anyway:

> We commence to build upon it a whole confused congeries of borrowed, faked, pilfered romanticisms, building a crumbling gothic into a masonry of honest brown stone, or foisting colonial porticos upon facades of Montpelier granite.[3]

1. Jesse Crisler and Joseph R. McElrath, Jr., *Frank Norris: A Reference Guide*, p. xiii.
2. "Frank Norris," p. 776.
3. "An American School of Fiction? A Denial."

Bibliography

Works by Frank Norris

Books

The Complete Edition of Frank Norris. 10 vols. Garden City, N.Y.: Doubleday, Doran & Co., 1928.

Frank Norris of "The Wave." San Francisco: Westgate Press, 1931.

The Literary Criticism of Frank Norris. Edited by Donald Pizer. Austin: University of Texas Press, 1964.

A Novelist in the Making: A Collection of Student Themes and the Novels Blix and Vandover and the Brute. Edited by James D. Hart. Cambridge: Harvard University Press, 1970.

The Responsibilities of the Novelist. New York: Doubleday, Page & Co., 1903.

Letters, Documents, and Miscellaneous Items

"Crepusculum." Overland Monthly 19 (April 1892):347.

"The Elusive Criticisms Syndicated by Frank Norris." Edited by Joseph Katz. Proof 3 (1973):221–52.

"Frank Norris on the Purpose of McTeague." Edited by Mukhtar Ali Isani. American Notes & Queries 10 (1972):118.

"Frank Norris Petitions The President and Faculty of The University of California." Edited by Franklin Walker. In The Friends of the Bancroft Library (Berkeley: The Council of the Friends of the Bancroft Library, 1970):n.p.

The Letters of Frank Norris. Edited by Franklin Walker. San Francisco: Book Club of California, 1956.

"Notes, I." Berkeley, Calif. Bancroft Library. Frank Norris Collection.

"The Remaining Seven of Frank Norris' 'Weekly Letters.'" Edited by Richard Allan Davison. American Literary Realism 2 (Summer 1968):47–65.

"Ten Letters by Frank Norris." Edited by Donald Pizer. Quarterly News-letter of the Book Club of California 28 (Summer 1962):51–61.

Articles

Note: The following abbreviations are used to indicate which articles are reprinted in one of the collections of Frank Norris's articles: FNW (Frank Norris of "The Wave"); LCFN (The

Literary Criticism of Frank Norris); RN (*The Responsibilities of the Novelist*); and CE (*The Complete Edition of Frank Norris*). Where appropriate, I have also listed pseudonymns or other variations from Norris's usual practice of signing his articles "Frank Norris" or, less frequently, "F.N."

"The American Public and 'Popular' Fiction." Syndicated, 2 February 1903. Rpt. LCFN, pp. 126–28; RN, pp. 103–8.

"An American School of Fiction? A Denial." *Boston Evening Transcript*, 22 January 1902, p. 17. Rpt. LCFN, pp. 108–11; RN, pp. 193–200.

"Art Association Exhibit: Fall Work of the Local Artists on View at the Hopkins House." *Wave* 16 (27 November 1897):6. Signed "Justin Sturgis."

"Belasco On Plays: The Great Playwright Speaks of His Methods." *Wave* 16 (28 August 1897):10. Rpt. FNW, pp. 155–58.

"The 'Bombardment': How a San Francisco Essayist Made a Little Go a Long Way." *Wave* 16 (3 April 1897):5. Rpt. FNW, pp. 123–27. Signed "Julian Sturgis."

"A Cat and Dog Life: Leonidas, and His Views upon the Members of His Troupe," *Wave* 16 (7 August 1897):6.

"Fiction is Selection." *Wave* 16 (11 September 1897):3. Rpt. LCFN, pp. 50–53. Signed "Justin Sturgis."

"Frank Norris' Weekly Letter." *Chicago American Art and Literary Review*, 8 June 1901, p. 5. Rpt. LCFN, pp. 8–10.

"Frank Norris' Weekly Letter." *Chicago American Art and Literary Review*, 22 June 1901, p. 8. Rpt. LCFN, pp. 182–86.

"Frank Norris' Weekly Letter." *Chicago American Art and Literary Review*, 13 July 1901, p. 8. Rpt. LCFN, pp. 53–55.

"The French Opera: Characteristics of the Troupe as Revealed in 'L'Africaine.' " *Wave* 16 (13 March 1897):11. Signed "F. L."

"Holiday Literature: The Chinese and California Girl Calendars —Remington's Great Sketches." *Wave* 16 (11 December 1897):8. Unsigned.

"Hunting Human Game: How Watch and Wait is Kept for the 'Swanhilda.' " *Wave* 16 (23 January 1897):4. Rpt. FNW, pp. 118–22.

"In the Compound of a Diamond Mine." *San Francisco Chronicle*, 2 February 1896, p. 10. Rpt. CE 10:223–29.

"Italy in California: The Vineyards of the Italian Swiss Colony at Asti." *Wave* 15 (24 October 1896):9.

" 'The Literature of the West': A Reply to W. R. Lighton." *Boston Evening Transcript*, 8 January 1902, p. 7. Rpt. LCFN, pp. 104–7.

"The Mechanics of Fiction." *Boston Evening Transcript*, 4 December 1901, p. 22. Rpt. LCFN, pp. 58–61; RN, pp. 147–54.

[Note on the Winter 1896 Exhibition at the Hopkins House]. *Wave* 15 (12 December 1896):4.

"Novelists of the Future: The Training They Need." *Boston Evening Transcript*, 27 November 1901, p. 14. Rpt. LCFN, pp. 10–14; RN, pp. 203–10.

"The Opinions of Leander: 'Holdeth Forth Upon Our Boys and the Ways of Them.'" *Wave* 16 (24 July 1897):7. Signed "Justin Sturgis."

"Our Unpopular Novelists: Disappearance of American Fiction From The Book Stores." *Wave* 14 (5 October 1895):7. Rpt. LCFN, pp. 25–28.

"Pictures To Burn: A Slim and Dreary Art Exhibition at the Hopkins House." *Wave* 16 (1 May 1897):4. Signed "Justin Sturgis."

"A Plea for Romantic Fiction." *Boston Evening Transcript*, 18 December 1901, p. 14. Rpt. LCFN, pp. 75–78; RN, pp. 213–20.

"A Problem in Fiction: Truth Versus Accuracy." *Boston Evening Transcript*, 6 November 1901, p. 20. Rpt. LCFN, pp. 55–58; RN, 223–28.

"A Question of Ideals: The American Girl of 1896 as Seen by Wenzel and by Gibson." *Wave* 15 (26 December 1896):7. Rpt. LCFN, pp. 166–68.

"Re-Creating a University: The Great Project of Reconstructing the College at Berkeley." *Wave* 15 (31 October 1896):5.

"The Responsibilities of the Novelist." *Critic* 41 (December 1902):537–40. Rpt. LCFN , pp. 94–98; RN, pp. 3–12.

"Student Life in Paris." *Collier's Weekly* 25 (12 May 1900):33.

"The True Reward of the Novelist." *World's Work* 2 (October 1901):1338. Rpt. LCFN, pp. 84–87; RN, pp. 15–22.

"Trilby and Princess Flavia: An Interviewer, Two Actresses, and Several Confidences." *Wave* 15 (10 October 1896):8.

"Western Types: An Art Student." *Wave* 15 (16 May 1896):10. Rpt. FNW, pp. 216–19.

"Why Women Should Write the Best Novels: And Why They Don't." *Boston Evening Transcript*, 13 November 1901, p. 20. Rpt. LCFN, 33–36; RN, pp. 231–38.

Secondary Sources

A.F.M. "Art Loan Exhibit." *Wave* 6 (7 March 1891):11.

Ahnebrink, Lars. *The Beginnings of Naturalism in American Fiction*. Upsala: A.-B. Lundequistska Bokhandeln, 1950.

Altschvl, A. "The Mark Hopkins Institute of Art." *Wave* 20 (31 March 1900):5.

"Another Gift From Collis P. Huntington: Keith's 'Summit of the Sierras,' Presented to the Art Association." *San Francisco Call*, 13 April 1900, p. 8.

Backus, Joseph M. "Gelett Burgess: A Biography of the Man Who Wrote 'The Purple Cow.'" Ph.D. dissertation, University of California, Berkeley, 1961.

Backus, Joseph M. ed. *Behind The Scenes: Glimpses of Fin de Siècle San Francisco.* San Francisco: Book Club of California, 1968.

Baird, Joseph Armstrong, Jr. *Time's Wondrous Changes: San Francisco Architecture, 1776–1915.* San Francisco: California Historical Society, 1962.

Barth, Gunther. "California Midwinter International Exposition." No. 2. San Francisco: Book Club of California, 1970.

Bauer, Walter John. "The Man-Woman Relationship in the Novels of Frank Norris." Ph.D. dissertation, New York University, 1973.

Berthoff, Warner. *The Ferment of Realism: American Literature, 1884–1919.* New York: Free Press, 1965.

Blitch, Janie Helen. "*The Pit* and Allusive Revelations." Master's thesis, University of Texas, 1970.

Budd, Louis J. "Objectivity and Low Seriousness in American Naturalism." In *Prospects*, edited by Jack Salzman, 1:41–61. New York: Burt Franklin and Co., 1975.

Burgess, Gelett. "Architectural Shams: The Efforts of San Francisco Architects to Achieve the Impossible." *Wave* 16 (20 March 1897):6.

———. *Bayside Bohemia: Fin de Siècle San Francisco and Its Little Magazines.* San Francisco: Book Club of California, 1954.

———. "Essays in Enthusiastic Journalism. III. 'Phyllida; or, The Milkmaid.'" *Academy* 57 (16 September 1899):290–91.

———. "The Night Reveries of an Exile." *Lark* 2, no. 15 (July 1896): n.p.

Burns, Stuart L. "The Rapist in Frank Norris's *The Octopus*." *American Literature* 42 (January 1971):567–69.

Cather, Willa. "Two Poets: Yone Noguchi and Bliss Carman." In *The World and the Parish: Willa Cather's Articles and Reviews, 1893–1902*, edited by William M. Curtin. 2:579–81. Lincoln: University of Nebraska Press, 1970.

Chase, Richard. *The American Novel and Its Tradition.* Garden City, N.Y.: Doubleday Anchor Books, 1957.

Childs, James. "The First Draft of *McTeague*, 1893." *American Notes & Queries* 3 (November 1964):37–38.

Cooperman, Stanley. "Frank Norris and the Werewolf of Guilt." *Modern Language Quarterly* 20 (September 1959):252–58.

Cosgrave, John O'Hara. "An Impression of Collis P. Huntington." *Wave* 20 (16 August 1900):12.

Crisler, Jesse, and McElrath, Joseph R., Jr. *Frank Norris: A Reference Guide*. Boston: G. K. Hall & Co., 1974.

Crow, Charles L. "The Real Vanamee and His Influence on Frank Norris' *The Octopus*." *Western American Literature* 9 (August 1974):131–39.

Dahlberg, Edward. "Stephen Crane: American Genius." In *The Leafless American*, edited by Harold Billings, pp. 58–61. Sausalito, Calif.: Roger Beacham, 1967.

Davison, Richard Allan. "Frank Norris' *The Octopus*: Some Observations on Vanamee, Shelgrim and St. Paul." In *Literature and Ideas in America*, edited by Robert Falk, pp. 182–203. Columbus: Ohio University Press, 1976.

Davison, Richard Allan, ed. *The Merrill Studies in The Octopus*. Columbus: Charles E. Merrill Publishing Co., 1969.

"The Decline of Poetry." *Wave* 12 (3 March 1894):9.

Dillingham, William B. *Frank Norris: Instinct and Art*. Lincoln: University of Nebraska Press, 1969.

Ditzler, Robert W. "Bohemianism in San Francisco At The Turn of the Century." Master's thesis, University of Washington, 1966.

Eames, Ninetta. "Jack London." *Overland Monthly* 35 (May 1900):417–25.

"Famous Pictures Owned on the West Coast, II." *Overland Monthly* 21 (February 1893):144–45.

Folsom, James K. "Social Darwinism or Social Protest? The 'Philosophy' of *The Octopus*." *Modern Fiction Studies* 8 (Winter 1962–1963):393–400.

———. "The Wheat and the Locomotive: Norris and Naturalistic Esthetics." In *American Literary Naturalism: A Reassessment*, edited by Yoshinobu Hakutani and Lewis Fried, pp. 57–74. Anglistische Forshungen, 109. Heidelberg: Carl Winter, 1975.

Fowlie, Wallace. *Mallarmé*. Chicago: University of Chicago Press, 1953.

French, Warren. *Frank Norris*. Twayne United States Authors Series, vol. 25. New York: Twayne, 1962.

Fried, Lewis. "The Golden Brotherhood of *McTeague*." *Zeitschrift für Anglistik und Amerikanistik* 23 (January 1975): 36–40.

Gardner, Joseph H. "Dickens, Romance, and *McTeague*: A Study in Mutual Interpretation." *Essays in Literature* (Western Illinois) 1 (1974):69–82.

"Gelett Burgess in Odd Skins." *San Francisco Call*, 11 May 1897, p. 9.

Goldman, Suzy Bernstein. "*McTeague*: The Imagistic Network." *Western American Literature* 7 (1972):83–99.

Graham, D. B. "Frank Norris, Actor." *Quarterly News-letter of the Book Club of California* 41 (Spring 1976):38–40.

———. "Yone Noguchi's 'Poe Mania.'" *Markham Review* 4 (May 1974):58–60.

Grassi, Luigi. *All the Sculpture of Donatello*. 2 vols. Translated by Paul Colacicci. New York: Hawthorne Books, 1964.

Greene, Clay M., ed. *The Annals of the Bohemian Club*. 5 vols. San Francisco: Bohemian Club, 1930.

Hart, James D. "Frank Norris." In *Homes of California Authors*, edited by Albert Shumate and Oscar Lewis, n.p. San Francisco: Book Club of California, 1967.

———. Introduction to *The Pit*, by Frank Norris. Columbus, Ohio: Charles E. Merrill, 1970.

———. *The Popular Book: A History of America's Literary Taste*. Berkeley: University of California, 1961.

Hawthorne, Julian. *Shapes That Pass: Memories of Old Days*. London: John Murray, 1928.

Hill, John S. "The Writing and Publication of the Novels of Frank Norris." *American Notes & Queries* 2 (June 1964): 151–52.

Hoffman, Charles G. "Norris and the Responsibility of the Novelist." *South Atlantic Quarterly* 54 (October 1955):508–15.

Hogan, Elodie. "Hills and Corners of San Francisco." *Californian Illustrated Magazine* 5 (December 1893):63–71.

Howells, W. D. "Frank Norris." *North American Review* 175 (December 1902):769–78.

Hubert, Gerard, and Serullaz, Maurice, eds. *Barye: Sculptures, Peintures et Aquarelles*. Paris: The Louvre, 1956.

Huysmans, J.-K. *Oeuvres Completes de J.-K. Huysmans*. 18 vols. Paris: Les Editions G. Crès et C., 1929.

"Is San Francisco A Sink of Iniquity?" *Wave* 14 (16 November 1895):1.

James, Henry. "The Art of Fiction." In *The Future of the Novel*, edited by Leon Edel, pp. 3–27. New York: Vintage Books, 1956.

———. *The Bostonians*. 1896. Reprint. New York: Random House, 1956.

———. *The Portrait of a Lady.* 1884. Reprint. Riverside Edition, edited by Leon Edel. New York: Houghton Mifflin, 1963.

Jeune, A. "An End To The Lark: The Brief History of a Freak Among Freaks." *Wave* 16 (10 April 1897):8.

Johnson, George W. "Frank Norris and Romance." *American Literature* 33 (March 1961):52–63.

———. "The Frontier Behind Frank Norris' *McTeague.*" *Huntington Library Quarterly* 26 (1962): 91–104.

Katz, Joseph. "Eroticism in American Literary Realism." *Studies in American Fiction* 5 (Spring 1977):35–50.

———. "The Shorter Publications of Frank Norris: A Checklist." *Proof* 3 (1973):155–220.

Katz, Joseph, and Manning, John J. "Notes on Frank Norris's Revision of Two Novels." *Papers of the Bibliographical Society of America* 62 (Second Quarter, 1968):256–59.

Keeler, Charles. "Friends Bearing Torches: A Company of Great-Hearted Californians." Unpublished typescript, 1939. Charles Keeler Collection, Bancroft Library, Berkeley, Calif.

———. *San Francisco and Thereabout.* San Francisco: A. M. Robertson, 1906.

Kelley, W. "Books and Bookmakers." *San Francisco Call,* 24 January 1897, p. 23.

Kirker, Harold. *California's Architectural Frontier: Style and Tradition in the Nineteenth Century.* San Marino, Calif.: The Huntington Library, 1960.

Le Petit Journal des Refusees, no. 1 (1 July 1896):n.p.

Levy, Harriet Lane. "Art Critics' Guide." *Wave* 6 (28 March 1891):11.

Lewis, Oscar. *The Big Four.* New York: Alfred A. Knopf, 1941.

London, Jack. "The Octopus." In *Jack London: American Rebel,* edited by Philip Foner, pp. 507–11. New York: Citadel Press, 1947.

Love, Glen A. "Frank Norris's Western Metropolitans." *Western American Literature* 11 (May 1976):3–22.

Lundy, Robert D. "The Making of *McTeague* and *The Octopus.*" Ph.D. dissertation, University of California, Berkeley, 1956.

Lynn, Kenneth. Introduction to *The Octopus,* by Frank Norris. Boston: Houghton Mifflin, 1958.

McElrath, Joseph R., Jr. "The Comedy of Frank Norris's *McTeague.*" *Studies in American Humor* 2 (October 1975): 88–95.

———. "Frank Norris's *Vandover and the Brute*: Narrative Technique and the Socio-Critical Viewpoint." *Studies in American Fiction* 4 (Spring 1976):27–43.

McEwen, Arthur. "The Plain People: How They Behave on the Sunday Picnic Boat When At Play." *Wave* 9 (16 July 1892): 25.

McKee, Irving. "Notable Memorials to Mussel Slough." *Pacific Historical Review* 17 (February 1948):19–27.

Mallarmé, Stéphane. *Poésies*. Édition Complete. Paris: Gallimard, 1945.

Marchand, Ernest. *Frank Norris: A Study*. Stanford: Stanford University Press, 1942.

Markham, Charles Edwin. "California at the World's Fair." *Californian Illustrated Magazine* 4 (November 1893):764–70.

Markham, Edwin. *The Man With The Hoe*. With Notes by the Author. New York: Doubleday, 1900.

———. *The Man With The Hoe*. New York: Doxey's At The Sign Of The Lark, 1899.

Marlow, Will A. *California Sketches*. Cincinnati: Editor Publishing Co., 1900.

Martin, Leslie. "Paintings at the Midwinter Fair." *Wave* 12 (17 March 1894):11.

Martin, Willard E., Jr. "Frank Norris's Reading at Harvard College." *American Literature* 8 (May 1935):203–4.

Millard, Bailey. "San Francisco in Fiction." *Bookman* 31 (August 1910):585–97.

Milne, Robert Duncan. "The Artist's Spectre." *Wave* 7 (21 June 1891):13.

Moers, Ellen. "The Finesse of Dreiser." *American Scholar* 33 (1964):109–14.

The "Monarch" Souvenir of Sunset City and Sunset Scenes. Being Views of California Midwinter Fair and Famous Scenes in the Golden State. San Francisco: H. S. Crocker Co. [1894?]

Nabokov, Vladimir. "Poshlust." In *A Writer's Reader*, edited by Donald Hall and D. L. Emblen, pp. 127–31. Boston: Little, Brown and Company, 1976.

"The Native Son Monument." *Wave* 16 (11 September 1897):9.

Noguchi, Yone. "The Invisible Night." *Lark* 2, no. 15 (July 1896):n.p.

———. "Love." *Wave* 16 (25 December 1897):7.

———. *The Story of Yone Noguchi*. Philadelphia: George W. Jacobs & Co., 1914.

The Orpheum & Entr'Acte Entertainer Programme 1, no. 2 (13 May 1895):n.p.

Orpheum Programme. 8 June 1896, n.p.

Orpheum Programme. 13 June 1896, n.p.

The Orpheum Programme. 28 December 1896, n.p.

"Paintings Like Keith's." *San Francisco Call*, 1 May 1896, p. 16.

Peixotto, Ernest C. "Architecture in San Francisco." *Overland Monthly* 21 (May 1893):449–63.

Pizer, Donald. "The Masculine-Feminine Ethic in Frank Norris' Popular Novels." *Texas Studies in Literature and Language* 6 (1964):84–91.

———. *The Novels of Frank Norris*. Bloomington: Indiana University Press, 1966.

———. "The Problem of Philosophy In The Novel." *Bucknell Review* 18 (Spring 1970):53–62.

Polk, Willis. "The 'Artists' Choice,' or, Why the Hibernia Bank and the Huntington House Are the Most Beautiful Buildings in San Francisco." *Wave* 9 (1 October 1892):8.

———. "How To Beautify San Francisco." *Wave* 21 (10 March 1900):4.

———. "San Francisco Beautiful." *Wave* 19 (April 15, 1899):3.

———. "The University Competition: A Critique." *Wave* 15 (7 November 1896):3.

Porter, Bruce. "The Beginning of Art in California." In *Art in California*, pp. 21–32. San Francisco: R. L. Bernier, 1916.

———. "Hail To Thee, Blithe Spirit." *Lark* 1, no. 1 (May 1895): n.p.

———. "The Winter Exhibition: The Hopkins House a Failure as an Art Gallery." *Wave* 15 (12 December 1896):4.

Rexroth, Kenneth. Afterword to *McTeague*, by Frank Norris. New York: New American Library, 1964.

Robinson, Peter. "Peixotto and his Work." *Out West* 19 (August 1903):133–45.

San Francisco Art Association. *Spring Exhibition*. 1896. n.p.

Scarabeus. "Spring Art." *Wave* 14 (27 April 1895):12.

Schneider, Robert W. "Frank Norris: The Naturalist as Victorian." *Midcontinent American Studies Journal* 3 (Spring 1962):13–27.

Sheppard, Keith S. "A New Note for McTeague's Canary." *Western American Literature* 9 (November 1974):217–18.

"Some Gems of Art Painted for the Fall Exhibition." *San Francisco Call*, 29 November 1896, p. 17.

"Splashes." *Wave* 8 (6 February 1892):7.

"Splashes." *Wave* 14 (20 April 1895):11.

Stirling, Monica. *The Fine and the Wicked: The Life and Times of Ouida*. New York: Coward-McCann, 1958.

"Things and People." *Wave* 16 (30 January 1897):7.

"Things and People." *Wave* 20 (9 December 1899):9.

Turner, Amy Lee. "Milton and Millet." *Studies By Members of SCMLA* 30 (Winter 1970):223–27.

[untitled]. *Wave* 15 (25 July 1896):9.

Vance, William L. "Romance in *The Octopus*." *Genre* 3 (June 1970):111–36.

Vidal, Gore. "American Plastic: The Matter of Fiction." *New York Review of Books* 23 (15 July 1976):31–37.

Walcutt, Charles C. *American Literary Naturalism: A Divided Stream*. Minneapolis: University of Minnesota Press, 1956.

————. "The Naturalism of *Vandover and the Brute*." In *Forms of Modern Fiction*, edited by William Van O'Connor, pp. 254–68. Minneapolis: University of Minnesota Press, 1948.

Walker, Franklin. *Frank Norris, A Biography*. 1932. Reprint. New York: Russell & Russell, 1963.

Walter, John I. "The San Francisco Art Association." In *Art in California*, pp. 97–101. San Francisco: R. L. Bernier, 1916.

Watson, Charles S. "A Source For The Ending of *McTeague*." *American Literary Realism* 5 (Spring 1972):173–74.

Wells, Carolyn. "The Latest Thing in Poets." *Critic* 29 (14 November 1896):302.

Wharton, Edith, and Codman, Ogden. *The Decoration of Houses*. New York: Charles Scribner's, 1897.

"Yone Noguchi." *Nation* 113 (7 December 1921):666–67.

"Yone Noguchi, the Japanese Poet, is Defended from a Charge of Plagiarism." *San Francisco Call*, 29 November 1896, p. 21.

Ziff, Larzer. *The American 1890s: Life and Times of a Lost Generation*. New York: Viking Press, 1966.

Index